STUDY GUIDE & DEVOTIONAL
YOUR CATALYST FOR GROWTH

RELENTLESS

JOHN
BEVERE

Relentless Study Guide & Devotional
Copyright © 2011 by Messenger International

WRITTEN AND EDITED BY:
Vincent M. Newfield
New Fields & Company
P. O. Box 622 • Hillsboro, Missouri 63050
www.preparethewaytoday.org

COVER, INTERIOR DESIGN & PRINT PRODUCTION:
Eastco Multi Media Solutions, Inc.
3646 California Rd. • Orchard Park, NY 14127
www.eastcomultimedia.com

Design Manager: Aaron La Porta
Designer: Heather Huether

Printed in Canada

TABLE OF CONTENTS

Welcome to the Relentless Experience

We are so excited that you have chosen to join us in this journey. Many hours of prayer, research, and preparation have been given to create an in-depth, interactive, and life-giving experience for you. This study guide has been designed to help establish truth and increase revelation in your life. Each of the following twelve chapters corresponds to a DVD session and contains thought-provoking questions, helpful definitions, and optional daily devotions.

Each chapter also includes...
- Life-changing **Scriptures**

- Insightful quotes from Christian leaders to aid in **Setting the Pace**

- **Core Strengtheners** of truth to remember from each session

- Weekly **challenges** to help you practically apply the principles of each session

Take time to meditate on these highlighted features.

We have also provided a **Session Summary** and a place to record your personal **notes**—all in an effort to help you experience the fullness of what God has for you in this study. Our prayer is not just to communicate information but to see God bring transformation in your life.

The Relentless Experience Online

Remember your leaders who taught you the word of God. Think of all the good that has come from their lives, and follow the example of their faith.
—Hebrews 13:7 NLT

There are many men and women of God who are powerful examples of relentless faith. To share their insights and experiences with you, we asked some of these leaders from around the world to provide their responses to certain questions from this study guide.

Throughout this guide, you will see questions marked with a 🖵 . Visit **RelentlessOnline.org** to watch video responses from leaders to these questions.

For more on this message, follow John Bevere on **facebook**. and **twitter**.

We also encourage you to...

- **Begin and end with prayer.** Invite the Holy Spirit to reveal and seal His truth in your heart.

- **Pace yourself** and develop a plan to complete each session during the week or allotted time.

- **Be consistent and committed** to the time and place you choose to do your study, and don't quit.

- **Be honest** with yourself and God as you answer questions. Truthfulness brings you freedom.

Suggestions for Group Leaders

Leaders, thank you for partnering with us to bring life-transforming truth to God's people. It is an honor to serve with you.

To help your group receive the most from this curriculum, we encourage each person to get a book and study guide. This allows for personal, in-depth study and reflection. Something special happens when we personally invest our time and thoughts in a teaching. We learn in ways that cannot be otherwise experienced. This study guide will challenge individuals to grow in their walk with God and to apply biblical principles to their personal lives.

How to use the Relentless Experience: We recommend that you ask students to read the book chapters before you gather. Watch or listen to a session together, then discuss selected questions from the study guide. Questions marked with a G are recommended for great group discussion. However, we want you to allow the Holy Spirit to lead in any direction He chooses. If you are not able to get through all of the material during your allotted group time, then encourage your group to complete the study guide chapter during the remainder of the week.

Our prayer is that your life and the life of each participant will be enriched and eternally changed by this study. May you experience the *Relentless* life God has called you to!

*You have need of steadfast patience and **endurance**, so that you may perform and fully accomplish the will of God, and thus receive and carry away [and enjoy to the full] what is promised.*

—Hebrews 10:36 AMP

Chapter **1**

RELENTLESS

Please refer to session 1 of the teaching series, along with the
introduction and chapters 1 and 2 in the Relentless book.

G 1. *Relentless* is a powerful word. It paints a picture
of persistence, endurance, and uncompromis-
ing, unyielding determination. When you hear
these words, what images come to mind?

Name a person who has shown relentless
courage to help better your life. How have they
made a difference, and how has their invest-
ment motivated you to help others?

Mom, Joni, Leita Mae, Ms-Nao,
Dr. Carr,

CORE STRENGTHENER

God is for you, and no one
wants you to have success
in the life of faith more than
Him. He's prepared a fabu-
lous life for you and fore-
sees a great finish in which
you leave a legacy of faith,
significance, and greatness
to benefit others. But it's all
contingent upon you being
a relentless believer.

RELENTLESS

Relentless describes an attitude or posture that is resolute, persistent, and
unyielding. Simply put, it does not relent—it does not slacken, become lenient
or concede. **Synonyms** that help define *relentless* are "adamant, rigorous,
uncompromising, unstoppable, tenacious, and determined." Other descrip-
tions include "constant, gritty, single-minded, steadfast, and enduring."

G 2. In the vision of the man in the rowboat, three types of people are depicted:
the *unbeliever* who flows with the current of the world; the *believer* who

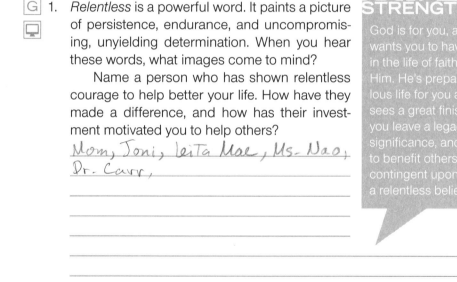

continues to press against the way of the world; and the *deceived* who has a "Christian" appearance but is flowing in the same direction as the world. Which description do you think best fits you? Why?

The believer

3. If you have a *pattern* of not finishing what you start, stop and look at the times you have quit in the past. What circumstances and conditions seem to resurface? *Pray* and ask God to show you your root reasons for wanting to quit.

SETTING *the* PACE

"Our pace, the incessant activity, the noise, the interruptions, the deadlines and demands, the daily schedule, and the periodic feelings of failure and futility bombard our beings like the shelling of a beachhead. Our natural tendency is to wave a white flag, shouting, 'I give up! I surrender!' This, of course, is the dangerous extreme of being weary—the decision to bail out, to throw in the towel, to give in to discouragement and give up. There is nothing wrong with feeling weary, but there is everything wrong with abandoning ship in the midst of the fight."
—*Charles Swindoll*[1]

Search me, O God, and know my heart; test me and know my anxious thoughts. Point out anything in me that offends you, and lead me along the path of everlasting life.
—Psalm 139:23-24 NLT

4. Being strong in faith empowers us to live relentlessly and make a difference in the world around us. What activities or practices are you presently doing that *strengthen* your faith in God and excite you to believe what He says? How can you do them more frequently?

The strong spirit of a man sustains him in bodily pain or trouble, but a weak and broken spirit who can raise up or bear?
—Proverbs 18:14 AMP

G 5. God powerfully declares in His Word that "...all who receive God's abundant grace and are freely put right with Him will **rule in life** through Christ" (Romans 5:17 TEV). Do you believe this statement? What does it mean to *rule in life*?

_____

_____

_____

_____

_____

G 6. Read Genesis 1:28, Psalm 115:16, and Romans 11:29. When situations become difficult, unfavorable, or even life-threatening, some believers default to the statement, "God is in control." What do you think about this response in light of God's Word?

_____

_____

_____

_____

> *God created human beings, making them to be like himself.*
> *He created them male and female, blessed them, and said,*
> *"Have many children, so that your descendants will live all over the*
> *earth and bring it under their control. **I am putting you in charge.**"*
> —Genesis 1:27-28 TEV

G 7. A huge problem arose when Adam and Eve sinned in the Garden of Eden, but God had a plan from before the beginning of time to set things right through the birth, death, and resurrection of His Son, Jesus. In your own words, briefly describe what happened to man's authority on earth when these events occurred:

In the Garden: Adam and Eve's Rebellion

_____

_____

_____

Christ's Resurrection

_____

_____

_____

CORE STRENGTHENER

Jesus was born of a woman, making Him 100 percent Man. He was fathered by the Holy Spirit, making Him 100 percent God, thus free from the curse of sin. Philippians 2:7 states, "When the time came, he set aside the privileges of deity and took on the status of a slave, became human! Having become human, he stayed human. It was an incredibly humbling process." (The Message)

8. Why did Jesus have to be born in a human body as the "Son of Man," and—according to Hebrews 2:17-18—what blessings have we received through His becoming "one of us"?

> So it is evident that it was essential that He be made like His brethren in every respect, in order that He might become a merciful (sympathetic) and faithful High Priest in the things related to God, to make atonement and propitiation for the people's sins. For because He Himself [in His humanity] has suffered in being tempted (tested and tried), He is able [immediately] to run to the cry of (assist, relieve) those who are being tempted and tested and tried [and who therefore are being exposed to suffering].
> —*Hebrews 2:17-18 AMP*

_____

_____

_____

Group leader extra: Hebrews 4:15-16

SETTING *the* PACE

"The church is the body of Christ, while Christ is the Head of the church. The relationships of parents and children, masters and servants, and even husbands and wives may all be severed, but *the physical head and its body are inseparable*; they are **forever one**. In like manner, Christ and the church too can never be sundered apart."
—***Watchman Nee***[3]

9. Who do you usually think of when you hear the word *Christ*? Carefully meditate on the scriptures below and explain what they speak to you about who "Christ" is and *who you are* in relation to Him as a believer.

> A body is made up of many parts, and each of them has its own use. That's how it is with us. There are many of us, but we each are part of the body of Christ, as well as part of one another.
> —*Romans 12:4-5 CEV*

> Don't you realize that your bodies are actually parts of Christ?
> —*1 Corinthians 6:15 NLT*

> Now all of you together are Christ's body, and each of you is a separate and necessary part of it.
> —*1 Corinthians 12:27 NLT*

The source of life, Christ, who puts us together in one piece, whose very breath and blood flow through us. He is the Head and we are the body. We can grow up healthy in God only as he nourishes us.

—Colossians 2:19 The Message

10. In addition to Christ becoming one of us, we have become *one with Him*. Through the new birth, the divine seed of Almighty God is implanted in us, and we become a brand-new creation *in Christ*. Take a few moments to meditate on the verses below and describe what the awesome privilege of being one in Christ means to you.

> For all of you who were baptized into Christ have clothed yourselves with Christ. There is neither Jew nor Greek, slave nor free, male nor female, for you are all *one in Christ Jesus*. If you belong to Christ, then you are Abraham's seed, and heirs according to the promise.
>
> *—Galatians 3:27-29 NIV*

CORE STRENGTHENER

We are Christ's body! Each of us is a various part. Jesus is the head, we are the rest; it's that simple! So when you read "Christ" in the New Testament, you need to see yourself in the mix, not just the One who died on the cross. We are *in* Christ. We *are* Christ! We are His body! We are *one* with Him!

By his divine power, *God has given us everything we need for living a godly life*. We have received all of this by coming to know him, the one who called us to himself by means of his marvelous glory and excellence. And because of his glory and excellence, he has given us great and precious promises. These are the promises that enable you to share his divine nature and escape the world's corruption caused by human desires.

—2 Peter 1:3-4 NLT

No one born (begotten) of God [deliberately, knowingly, and habitually] practices sin, for *God's nature abides in him* [His principle of life, the divine sperm, remains permanently within him]; and he cannot practice sinning because he is born (begotten) of God.

—1 John 3:9 AMP

Group leader extras: John 3:3-8, 15-21; 2 Corinthians 5:17, 21; Galatians 2:20; 1 Peter 1:23.

SETTING *the* PACE

"As husband and wife are one, so is Jesus one with all those who are united to Him by faith—they are one by a conjugal union that can never be broken. More than this, *believers are members of the body of Christ*, and so *they are one with Him* by a loving, living, lasting union. God has called us into this union, this fellowship, this partnership. ...Because we are one with Jesus, we are made partakers of His nature and are endowed with His immortal life. Our destiny is linked with that of our Lord, and until He can be destroyed, it is not possible that we would perish."
—*Charles Spurgeon* [4]

Weekly CHALLENGE

Choose a specific goal to meet for the duration of this study. Select a daily or weekly goal for your spiritual life, health, relationships, finances, or another challenging area. Whether you choose to complete this goal alone, with your family, or in a group of friends, commit to maintain this practice throughout the next twelve weeks.

My personal Relentless challenge:

_____

_____

_____

_____

_____

_____

_____

_____

_____

_____

_____

Group leader extra: Decide on a goal to be completed by everyone in your group.

Day 1 CROSSING THE FINISH LINE

I have fought the good fight, I have finished the race, and I have remained faithful.
—2 Timothy 4:7 NLT

There is a big difference between starting and finishing. When we start something, we are usually fresh, eager, energetic, and ready to tackle anything. By the time we reach the end, we are often emotionally and physically spent. If there was anyone who could identify with this, it was the apostle Paul. Yet to him, the end of the course was always in sight, and finishing it well was very important. In spite of all the troubles he faced, Paul said,

"But **none of these things move me**; neither do I esteem my life dear to myself, if only I may *finish my course with joy* and the ministry which I have obtained from [which was entrusted to me by] the Lord Jesus, faithfully to attest to the good news (Gospel) of God's grace (His unmerited favor, spiritual blessing, and mercy)."
—Acts 20:24 AMP

Finishing strong was also important to Jesus. He said, "My nourishment comes from doing the will of God, who sent me, and from *finishing* his work" (John 4:34 NLT). Just before going to the cross, He prayed, "I have glorified You on the earth. I have *finished* the work which You have given Me to do" (John 17:4 NKJV). When He was on the cross and His work was complete, He cried out, "It is *finished*" (John 19:30 NKJV).

What insights can you learn from Paul and our Lord Jesus to apply in your life?

What would be a fitting epitaph on your tombstone, a statement to sum up your life right now? If you're not satisfied with it, how would you live in order to change it?

Read Hebrews 12:1-3. How might keeping your *eyes on the eternal prize* help you finish on a good note? What can you gather from this passage to help you cross the finish line?

For Further Study...
1 Corinthians 9:24-27
1 Timothy 6:11-12
Ecclesiastes 7:8

Day 2 A TEST OF FAITH

Test yourselves to make sure you are solid in the faith. Don't drift along taking everything for granted. Give yourselves regular checkups. You need firsthand evidence, not mere hearsay, that Jesus Christ is in you. Test it out. If you fail the test, do something about it.

—2 Corinthians 13:5 The Message

If you are relentlessly walking with God, there will be evidence of His presence and power in your life. One of the best ways to confirm you are growing in Christ and not stagnant is to examine the fruit your life is producing. The true evidence that Jesus is living in and through you is that your life is producing His character.

Carefully read Galatians 5:19-23 and Ephesians 5:8-9. From these verses describing the *fruit of the flesh* and the *fruit of the Spirit*, what kind of fruit do you see in your life?

According to Jesus' words in John 15:1-8, what is the indispensable require-ment for you to produce the fruit of His character? What does this say to you personally?

Is the Holy Spirit prompting you to make any adjustments in your life? If so, what are they?

For Further Study...
Psalm 1; Psalm 92:12-15;
Jeremiah 17:7-8;
Matthew 13:23;
Mark 4:20; Luke 8:15

Day 3 BRACE YOURSELF

Lift up your tired hands, then, and strengthen your trembling knees! Keep walking on straight paths. ...Guard against turning back from the grace of God.
—Hebrews 12:12-15 TEV

Turning back from the grace of God is a sure sign that one has quit—that he or she is no longer pressing onward and upward in their relationship with the Lord.

Stop and think. What are the top two things going on in your life right now that make you feel like quitting—things that exhaust and discourage you, draining you of joy and strength? Is it financial pressures? Is it problems with your health? Are you struggling in a relationship? Regardless of your situation, God's Word can revolutionize your perspective. It will empower you to brace yourself for anything you are dealing with.

Using your Bible's concordance, look up the topics in which you are struggling—or do a *keyword search* for them online, using a website such as www. biblegateway.com. Explore the verses you find in a variety of translations. Write out and meditate on at least two scriptures that breathe new life into your heart and encourage you to press on.

_____ wears me out and makes me want to quit. But God says...

_____

_____

_____

_____

_____

_____ wears me out and makes me want to quit. But God says...

_____

_____

_____

_____

_____

For Further Study...
Here are some sample topics:

FINANCIAL PROVISION	HEALTH & HEALING	RECONCILED RELATIONSHIPS
2 Corinthians 9:8-12	Isaiah 53:5; 1 Peter 2:24	Psalm 133:1-3; Ephesians 4:2-3
Malachi 3:10; Proverbs 3:9-10	Psalm 107:20; Exodus 23:25-26	1 Corinthians 1:10
Luke 6:38; Philippians 4:19	Proverbs 4:20-22	Romans 12:18-21; 1 Peter 3:8-11

Day 4 THE ENEMY'S BEEN DEFEATED

For this purpose the Son of God was manifested, that He might destroy the works of the devil.

—I John 3:8 NKJV

Christ's victory on the cross gives us countless blessings. One that we must never forget is the defeat of our enemy. Through Jesus' death and resurrection, Satan and his demonic allies were dealt a fatal blow. The enemy *has been* defeated—it has already happened. It is not something we are waiting for; it has already taken place. As believers, we are fighting *from* a position of victory, not *for* it.

Evangelist and author **T.L. Osborn** was known across the globe for bringing the miraculous healing power of God to countless people. He said,

"Jesus' triumph was our triumph. His victory was our victory. He did nothing for Himself—He did it all for us. He defeated Satan for us. He spoiled his power for us. He destroyed his works for us. He conquered him for us.

...When Jesus arose from the dead, He left an eternally defeated Satan behind Him. Always think of Satan as an eternally defeated foe. Think of Satan as one over whom Jesus—and you in Jesus' name—have entire dominion and authority."[5]

Take a moment to ponder the truths in these verses:

Colossians 2:14-15 • Hebrews 2:14-15 & 1 John 5:18 • Revelation 12:11
Look them up in multiple translations and meditate on their message.

What happened to the enemy through Jesus' finished work? What else is the Lord showing you in these verses?

_____

_____

_____

Group leader extras: John 12:31-32, 16:33; Galatians 3:13; Colossians 1:13-14.

How does knowing the enemy is defeated encourage you and change your perspective?

_____

_____

_____

For Further Study...
Christ's victory has also destroyed the power of sin. Carefully meditate on the message of these passages.
Romans 6:2-8, 8:1-3; Galatians 2:20, 5:24; Colossians 3:3; 1 Peter 2:24

Day 5 **WHAT DO YOU BELIEVE?**

He touched their eyes and said, "What you have believed will be done for you!"
—Matthew 9:29 GW

The Bible is filled with many awesome promises, but if they are not met with faith in our hearts they remain nothing more than words on a page. We will never rise above the level of what we believe. Stop and chew on that statement: *We will never rise above the level of what we believe.* This is the principle of Proverbs 23:7: "For as he **thinks** in his heart, so is he" (NKJV). What we think is what we become.

Author and pastor Mark Batterson gives us a fresh perspective on the power of believing and what it takes to reshape our faith. He states...

"Half of learning is learning. The other half of learning is unlearning. ...Faith is unlearning the senseless worries and misguided beliefs that keep us captive. It is far more complex than simply modifying behavior. Faith involves synaptogenesis. Faith is rewiring the human brain. Neurologically speaking, that is what we do when we study Scripture. We are literally upgrading our minds by downloading the mind of Christ.

Just as a computer hard drive needs to be defragmented to optimize performance, our minds need to be defragmented. So how do we defragment our faith? How do we renew our minds? How do we get ourselves out of the mental pit we've gotten ourselves into? The way to upgrade your mind is to download Scripture."[6]

So what do you believe? Do you believe *you are Christ* in the earth? Do you believe *you are one with Him*? Do you believe *you are a partaker of His divine nature*—that His supernatural DNA is fixed within the fibers of your spirit? Do you believe that *the enemy has been defeated* and all authority is given to you through Christ to *rule in this life*? What you believe will be done for you!

Of all the truths presented in this session, which challenges you most? Why?

_____

_____

_____

Pray and surrender these things to God. Ask Him for grace to believe what He says is true.

Carefully read Romans 10:17, 12:2; Hebrews 4:12 and Colossians 3:16. In light of these verses, what is a good recipe for strengthening your faith?

For Further Study...
Matthew 21:18-22; Mark 11:20-25; John 6:28-29; Hebrews 11:1, 6; Romans 10:10-11

_____

_____

_____

Day 6 NOTHING IS IMPOSSIBLE WITH GOD!

I am the Lord! There is nothing too difficult for me.

—Genesis 18:14 CEV

It takes a relentless believer to see the impossible become possible. As we wholeheartedly and perseveringly put our faith and trust in the Lord and put no confidence in our flesh, we position ourselves to see the miraculous take place.

Anne Graham Lotz, daughter of evangelist Billy Graham, said, "When we face an impossible situation, all self-reliance and self-confidence must melt away; we must be totally dependent on Him for the resources."[7] As you journey through this study and yield yourself to God, you will learn how to face what is beyond your human ability and see the impossible become possible.

Meditate on the message of these powerful promises from God's Word.

Jesus looked at them and said, "With man this is impossible, but with God all things are possible."

—Matthew 19:26 NIV

"What do you mean, 'If I can'?" Jesus asked. "Anything is possible if a person believes."

—Mark 9:23 NLT

Jesus looked at them intently and said, "Humanly speaking, it is impossible. But not with God. Everything is possible with God."

—Mark 10:27 NLT

For with God nothing is ever impossible and no word from God shall be without power or impossible of fulfillment.

—Luke 1:37 AMP

As you meditate on these verses, what do they stir in your spirit?

What would you like to see happen—and believe is God's will—but think or feel is impossible?

Prayer

Father, I want to want nothing but You! I repent of being attached to the things of this world and going with its flow. Strengthen me to turn a deaf ear to its cries and the voices of the enemy and my flesh. As I journey through this study, create in me a relentless heart—a valiant, courageous, and determined spirit that won't let anything deter me from completing the assignments You give me. Forge within me a spirit of iron, strong in faith and promptly obedient to You. In Jesus' name, Amen.

SESSION SUMMARY

The Christian life is a like race. It is not a sprint but a long-distance marathon. To run effectively and finish the course God has set before us, we must develop a relentless spirit—one that never quits but tenaciously endures to the end. How do we live relentlessly and rule in life over all the opposition of the enemy? Through God's abundant grace available to us in Christ.

(1) Charles R. Swindoll, *Growing Strong in the Seasons of Life* (Portland, OR: Multnomah Press, 1983) p. 135. (2) Kenneth E. Hagin, *The Believer's Authority* (Tulsa, OK: RHEMA Bible Church, 2007) p. 39. (3) Watchman Nee, *Spiritual Authority* (New York, NY: Christian Fellowship Publishers, Inc., 1972) pp. 76-77. (4) Charles Spurgeon, *All of Grace* (New Kensington, PA: Whitaker House, 1981) pp. 162-163. (5) T.L. Osborn, *Healing the Sick* (Tulsa OK: Harrison House Inc., 1992) p. 111. (6) Mark Batterson, *In a Pit with a Lion on a Snowy Day* (Colorado Springs, CO: Multnomah Books, 2006) pp. 44-46. (7) *Fast Break, Five-Minute Devotions to Start Your Day* (Parable, 2007) Day 66.

Notes

Notes

All who receive God's abundant grace and are freely put right with him will **rule in life** *through Christ.*

—Romans 5:17 TEV

EMPOWERED TO RULE

Please refer to session 2 of the teaching series, along with chapters 2 and 3 in the Relentless book.

IMMEASURABLE • UNLIMITED • SURPASSING

Immeasurable means "cannot be measured; immense; beyond all ability to measure." *Unlimited* denotes "having no bounds or limits; unconfined; unrestrained." *Surpassing* indicates "going beyond all others; exceeding in quality; excellent in a distinguishing degree."[1] **Synonyms** include *infinite, massive, endless,* and *limitless.* All these words describe the power of God—His grace—that is at work *in* and **for** you who believe (see Ephesians 1:19).

---

1. As a believer, God's limitless power is always available to you. *Grace* is the power; the Holy Spirit living in you is the source. Can you remember a time when God's surpassing power came through for you? Describe what happened. In what current situation do you need to experience God's immeasurable greatness? How does remembering past victories strengthen your faith?

   God's power really came through when...

   _____

   _____

   _____

   _____

   Right now, I need God's unlimited power in...

   _____

   _____

   _____

   _____

Group leader extra: Psalm 77:11-15

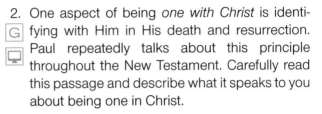

CORE STRENGTHENER

We are a part of Christ. Therefore, the exact power He has, we have! "As He [Jesus] is, so are we in this world" (1 John 4:17 NKJV). Let this soak deep into your heart.

2. One aspect of being *one with Christ* is identifying with Him in His death and resurrection. Paul repeatedly talks about this principle throughout the New Testament. Carefully read this passage and describe what it speaks to you about being one in Christ.

> Your old sin-loving nature was buried with him by baptism when he died, and when God the Father, with glorious power, brought him back to life again, you were given his wonderful new life to enjoy. For you have become a part of him, and so you died with him, so to speak, when he died; and now you share his new life, and shall rise as he did.
>
> Your old evil desires were nailed to the cross with him; that part of you that loves to sin was crushed and fatally wounded, so that your sin-loving body is no longer under sin's control, no longer needs to be a slave to sin; for when you are deadened to sin you are freed from all its allure and its power over you.
>
> So look upon your old sin nature as dead and unresponsive to sin, and instead be alive to God, alert to him, through Jesus Christ our Lord.
>
> —Romans 6:4-7, 11 TLB

Group leader extras: Galatians 5:24-25; Colossians 2:11-14, 3:3.

CORE STRENGTHENER

We are Christ's body. The moment we were immersed into Him, our history changed. We died with Him, were buried with Him and were raised with Him. And as brand-new beings, we live as He does! "As He is, so are we in this world." We are *in* Christ. We *are* Christ! We are *one* with Him!

I have been crucified with Christ [in Him I have shared His crucifixion]; it is no longer I who live, but Christ (the Messiah) lives in me; and the life I now live in the body I live by faith in (by adherence to and reliance on and complete trust in) the Son of God, Who loved me and gave Himself up for me.
—Galatians 2:20 AMP

3. In addition to being crucified with Christ, we have also been raised up with Him and seated in heavenly places. Carefully meditate on Jesus' powerful words in Matthew and Luke and God's declaration through Paul in Ephesians. In light of these verses, how would you describe your **authority** as a believer? Do you see anything you haven't seen before?

All authority has been given to Me in heaven and on earth. Go therefore and make disciples of all the nations, baptizing them in the name of the Father and of the Son and of the Holy Spirit, teaching them to observe all things that I have commanded you; and lo, I am with you always, even to the end of the age.

—Matthew 28:18-20 NKJV

Behold! I have given you authority and power to trample upon serpents and scorpions, and [physical and mental strength and ability] over all the power that the enemy [possesses]; and nothing shall in any way harm you.

—Luke 10:19 AMP

And {God} raised us up together with Him and made us sit down together [giving us joint seating with Him] in the heavenly sphere [by virtue of our being] in Christ Jesus (the Messiah, the Anointed One).

—Ephesians 2:6 AMP

{God} raised Him from the dead and seated Him at His [own] right hand in the heavenly [places], far above all rule and authority and power and dominion and every name that is named [above every title that can be conferred], not only in this age and in this world, but also in the age and the world which are to come.

—Ephesians 1:20-21 AMP
{Words in brackets added for clarity.}

Group leader extras: Mark 6:7, Luke 9:1-6.

AUTHORITY

Authority is the power or right to perform certain acts without hindrance. It is based upon some form of law, whether divine, civil, or moral. Supreme authority is God's alone (Romans 13:1), therefore all human authority is derived from Him.

God's authority is unconditional and absolute (Psalm 2; 29:10; Proverbs 21:30; Isaiah 40). From His authority comes that of governments (John 19:10-11; Romans 13:1), parents (Ephesians 6:1-4), employers (Ephesians 6:5-9), church elders (Hebrews 13:7, 17), and other positions of power.

Because Jesus is God, His authority is not merely derived from the Father but is also inherent. *His power knows no limitations* and is the basis of His commission to us, His disciples (Mark 6:7, Matthew 28:18-20).[2]

4. Think for a moment. What things might cause G us to *relinquish our authority* at home, at work, or in our community? Are you currently facing any of these challenges? If so, how can God's grace empower you to deal with them?

_____

_____

_____

_____

_____

_____

5. To *rule in life* we need the empowerment of God's **grace**. First and foremost, grace is God's merciful, unmerited favor that provides us forgiveness of sin and salvation. Stop and honestly answer this vital question:

How am I saved: made acceptable, righteous, lovable, and in right relationship with God?

_____

_____

_____

_____

Group leader extras: Ephesians 1:7, 2:4-5, 8-9; Acts 15:11; Romans 11:5-6; Titus 2:11.

SETTING *the* **PACE**

"This grace of God is your strength, as it is your joy; and it is only by abiding in it that you can really live the life of the redeemed. Be strong, then, in this grace; draw your joy out of it; and beware how you turn to anything else for refreshment, or comfort, or holiness. ...Draw continually on Christ and His fullness for this grace."
—F. Horatius Bonar[5]

GRACE

The original Greek word for *grace* used exclusively in the New Testament is *charis*. In general, *grace* means "undeserved goodwill, loving-kindness, and favor." Equally important, grace carries with it the meaning of "**divine power**."[3] Dr. James Strong, a well-respected scholar who invested 35 years developing an exhaustive concordance of biblical words, said grace is "the divine influence upon the heart and its reflection in a person's life."[4] Essentially, grace is *God's free empowerment that gives us the ability to go beyond our natural ability.*

G 6. God's grace not only provides us salvation, but it also infuses us with the *fullness of Christ* Himself. His divine nature is deposited and developed in us by the work of His awesome Spirit. Take time to chew on these powerful verses and describe what it means to receive the *fullness of His grace.*

> For out of His fullness (abundance) we have all received [all had a share and we were all supplied with] one grace after another and spiritual blessing upon spiritual blessing and even favor upon favor and gift [heaped] upon gift.
>
> —*John 1:16 AMP*

> {Christ's} body, the fullness of Him Who fills all in all [for in that body {of Christ} lives the full measure of Him Who makes everything complete, and Who fills everything everywhere with Himself].
>
> —*Ephesians 1:23 AMP*

> For in {Christ} the whole fullness of Deity (the Godhead) continues to dwell in bodily form [giving complete expression of the divine nature]. And you are in Him, made full and having come to fullness of life [in Christ *you too are filled with the Godhead*—Father, Son and Holy Spirit—and reach full spiritual stature]. And He is the Head of all rule and authority [of every angelic principality and power].
>
> —*Colossians 2:9-10 AMP*
> {Italicized words in brackets added for clarity.}

Receiving the fullness of Christ means...

_____
_____
_____
_____
_____
_____
_____
_____

G 7. Romans 5:2 declares that *we have access by faith into God's grace in which we stand.* Carefully ponder these promises from Scripture and identify how we receive God's grace. What must we guard against so that the flow of grace isn't cut off?

> But He gives us more and more grace (power of the Holy Spirit, to meet this evil tendency and all others fully). That is why He says, God sets

SETTING the PACE

"*All true believers receive from Christ's fullness.* The best and greatest saints cannot live without Him, the weakest may live by Him. This excludes proud boasting, that we have nothing but we have received it; and silences perplexing fears, that we want nothing but we may receive it. Our receivings by Christ are all summed up in this one word, **grace**; so great a gift, so rich, so invaluable."

—***Matthew Henry***[6]

Himself against the proud and haughty, but gives grace [continually] to the lowly (those who are humble enough to receive it).

—James 4:6 AMP

God opposes the proud but gives grace to the humble.

—1 Peter 5:5 NIV

May God give you more and more grace and peace as you grow in your knowledge of God and Jesus our Lord. By his divine power, *God has given us everything we need for living a godly life.* We have received all of this by coming to know him, the one who called us to himself by means of his marvelous glory and excellence.

—2 Peter 1:2-3 NLT

_____

_____

_____

Group leader extras: 2 Corinthians 12:9; 2 Timothy 2:1.

SETTING *the* PACE

"*Prayer* is the exercise of drawing on the grace of God. Don't say—I will endure this until I can get away and pray. **Pray now**; *draw on the grace of God in the moment of need.* Prayer is the most practical thing, it is not the reflex action of devotion. Prayer is the...thing in which we learn to draw on God's grace."
—Oswald Chambers[7]

8. God's empowering grace is the most versatile source of strength we have. It takes the form of any provision we need. Like a master key, it opens the door to all of God's blessings, including wisdom, healing, direction, creativity, and miraculous power. Stop and think: What do you need God's grace to provide for you and your family right now?

I need God's grace to...

1._____

_____

2._____

_____

3._____

_____

My spouse/children need God's grace to...

1._____

_____

2._____

_____

3._____

_____

Get quiet before the Lord and ask Him for His grace in these specific areas. Search His Word for His promised provision concerning these things. Meditate on and pray His promises. Then watch how He answers your prayers. Journal what happens so you can recall it and share with others.

"Here's what I want you to do: Find a quiet, secluded place so you won't be tempted to role-play before God. Just be there as simply and honestly as you can manage. The focus will shift from you to God, and you will begin to sense his grace. The world is full of so-called prayer warriors who are prayer-ignorant. They're full of formulas and programs and advice, peddling techniques for getting what you want from God. Don't fall for that nonsense. This is your Father you are dealing with, and he knows better than you what you need. With a God like this loving you, you can pray very simply."
—Matthew 6:6-8 The Message

9. Evidence of God's grace could clearly be seen working in and through Stephen, Paul, and the church at Antioch (see Acts 6:8, 11:22-23, 19:11). What are some outward evidences of God's grace working in your life? Ask others who are close to you what they see.

_____

_____

_____

_____

Group leader extras: 1 Peter 4:10-11

G 10. The tribe in Africa had been given an awesome gift, but they failed to utilize it because they didn't understand its primary function. Grace's primary function is **empowerment**—the ability to go beyond our natural ability. After going through this session, how do you see God's grace differently than you did before? What truth(s) did the Holy Spirit use to make the meaning of grace more real?

_____

_____

_____

_____

_____

Prayer for Empowerment

Father, may Christ through my faith [actually] dwell (settle down, abide, make His permanent home) in my heart! May I be rooted deep in love and founded securely on love, that I may have the power and be strong to apprehend and grasp with all the saints [God's devoted people, the experience of that love] what is the breadth and length and height and depth [of it].

May I really come to know [practically, through experience for myself] the love of Christ, which far surpasses mere knowledge [without experience]. May I be filled [through all my being] with all the fullness of You [may I have the richest measure of Your divine Presence, and become a body wholly filled and flooded with God Himself]! In Jesus name, Amen.

A personalized prayer based on Ephesians 3:17-19 (AMP).

Weekly CHALLENGE

One of the best ways to capture a new revelation is to teach it to someone else. Think of one or two people not in this study who you know are struggling to rule in an area of life by their own strength. Invite them to meet for coffee, go out on a shopping date, or come to your home for dinner, and share what you have learned about the grace of God as His empowerment for their situation.

Day 1 **ALL OF HEAVEN IS BEHIND YOU!**

What are all the angels? They are spirits sent to serve those who are going to receive salvation.

—Hebrews 1:14 GW

As believers, we are *saved* by grace and *empowered* by grace to *rule in this life*—to see God's kingdom manifest on earth as it is in heaven. God sent Jesus to represent Him, and Jesus sends us to represent Him. **Rick Renner**, an extraordinary pastor and student of Greek, captures this principle well. He says,

> "Did you know you have a high-ranking, esteemed, celebrated, impressive and influential job in the Kingdom of God? It's true! You are so important to the kingdom of God that all of Heaven is standing behind you, just waiting to back you up, defend you, provide for you, help and assist you, and join forces with your actions of faith! In short, Heaven is just waiting to act on your behalf. Why? Because **you are an ambassador** for Christ to this world!"[8]

You are an ambassador for Jesus Christ! You are empowered by His grace and backed by His angelic force to bring solutions to the problems of earth.

Stop and think. In what ways would you like to see yourself and God's people ruling in life?

_____

_____

What injustice in the world—specifically in your sphere of influence—frustrates and enrages you most?

_____

_____

Knowing that you have the power (grace) to change the situation, what will you do?

_____

_____

*For He will give His angels [especial] charge over you to **accompany** and **defend** and **preserve** you in all your ways [of obedience and service]. They shall bear you up on their hands, lest you dash your foot against a stone.*

—Psalm 91:11-12 AMP

For Further Study...
God's angelic forces have intervened for His people in some magnificent ways. Here are a few examples:
Israel: Exodus 23:20-23 **Elijah**: 1 Kings 19:3-8 **Daniel**: Daniel 6:16-23 **Peter**: Acts 12:5-11

Day 2 ARE YOU APPEALING?

*It was God [personally present] in Christ, reconciling and restoring the world to favor with Himself, not counting up and holding against [men] their trespasses [but cancelling them], and committing to us the message of reconciliation (of the restoration to favor). So we are Christ's ambassadors, God **making His appeal** as it were through us. We [as Christ's personal representatives] beg you for His sake to lay hold of the divine favor [now offered you] and be reconciled to God.*
—2 Corinthians 5:19-20 AMP

Through our faith in Christ Jesus—our belief that He was sinless, died to pay the penalty for our sin, and victoriously rose from the grave—we have been *reconciled* to God. We have been given a clean slate and are placed in right relationship with Him. And in our new relationship, God has appointed us to help others be reconciled to Him. He wants us to rule in life as His *ambassadors*.

WHAT IS AN AMBASSADOR?

In New Testament times, as well as today, the word *ambassador* carries the same meaning. An ambassador is...

- An official representative who is authorized to speak on behalf of his sender.
- An authorized messenger who has the power to make decisions and to represent the will of the government, nation, or king he represents
- A diplomatic agent of the highest rank accredited to a foreign government of king.

As an *ambassador* of Jesus Christ, you are His authorized representative on the earth through whom God is making His appeal to the people of the world to be put back in right relationship with Him.[9]

Imagine that you are *not* in a relationship with God, but you know someone who lives and behaves like you. Would this person draw you to Christ? Why or why not?

_____

_____

_____

Go deeper! Ask a close friend what they see in you that would or wouldn't draw them to Christ.

What changes can you make in the way you live to make the knowledge of God more appealing to those around you?

_____

_____

_____

_____

For Further Study...
Matthew 5:13-16;
1 Peter 2:9-17;
Luke 6:35

Day 3 HOW DO YOU SEE YOURSELF?

Therefore if any person is [ingrafted] in Christ (the Messiah) he is a new creation (a new creature altogether); the old [previous moral and spiritual condition] has passed away. Behold, the fresh and new has come!

—2 Corinthians 5:17 AMP

In order to effectively rule in life, you must learn to see God for who He is and see yourself as an inseparable part of Christ. You are **one** with Him and share in the miraculous power of His grace. This is why Paul passionately said, *My prayer is that light will flood your hearts and that you will understand the hope that was given to you when God chose you. Then you will discover the glorious blessings that will be yours together with all of God's people* (Ephesians 1:18 CEV). God wants to open the eyes of your heart...

[So that you can know and understand] what is the immeasurable and unlimited and surpassing greatness of His power *in and for us who believe*, as demonstrated in the working of His mighty strength,

Which He exerted in Christ when He raised Him from the dead and seated Him at His [own] right hand in the heavenly [places], far above all rule and authority and power and dominion and every name that is named [above every title that can be conferred], not only in this age and in this world, but also in the age and the world which are to come.

And He has put all things under His feet and has appointed Him the universal and supreme Head of the church [a headship exercised throughout the church], which is His body, the fullness of Him Who fills all in all [for in that body lives the full measure of Him Who makes everything complete, and Who fills everything everywhere with Himself].

—*Ephesians 1:19-23 AMP*

What does it mean that you are seated in a heavenly position of authority?

_____

_____

_____

_____

Do you believe these things about yourself? What else is God showing you?

_____

_____

_____

_____

CORE STRENGTHENER

Remember, you are part of Christ. The head is not cut off from the body. We are all together seated in a place of rulership, authority, and power in the heavenly sphere. In other words, we are in a sphere that is above any forces of this earth. In fact, we are *far above*! There is not one demon spirit, fallen angel, or even Satan himself who has power or authority over us. We reign supreme.

Day 4 YOU ARE GOD'S CHILD!

See what [an incredible] quality of love the Father has given (shown, bestowed on) us, that we should [be permitted to] be named and called and counted the children of God! And so we are!

—1 John 3:1 AMP

By grace we have been saved! God "has rescued us from the kingdom of darkness and transferred us into the Kingdom of his dear Son, who purchased our freedom and forgave our sins" (Colossians 1:13-14 NLT). Praise His Name! But God didn't just make us His servants. He adopted us and made us *joint heirs* with Jesus. Everything—everything—that is Jesus' is also ours. Ephesians 1:3 (GW) says, "Through Christ, God has blessed us with *every spiritual blessing* that heaven has to offer." What an amazing promise!

Meditate on the message of these verses:

But to all who believed him and accepted him, he gave the right to become children of God.

—John 1:12-13 NLT

For all who are led by the Spirit of God are children of God. So you have not received a spirit that makes you fearful slaves. Instead, you received God's Spirit when he adopted you as his own children. Now we call him, "Abba, Father." For his Spirit joins with our spirit to affirm that we are God's children.

—Romans 8:14-16 NLT

God sent him {Jesus} to buy freedom for us who were slaves to the law, so that he could adopt us as his very own children. ...God has sent the Spirit of his Son into your hearts, and now you can call God your dear Father. Now you are no longer a slave but God's own child. And since you are his child, everything he has belongs to you.

—Galatians 4:5-7 NLT

What is the Lord revealing to you about being His son/daughter?

Read Ephesians 5:1-2. What does this speak to you about being God's child?

Read 2 Peter 1:3-4. Describe the connection between having God's divine nature—the fullness of Christ—and being His child, a joint heir with Jesus.

Related Scriptures: Galatians 3:26-29; Ephesians 3:6

Day 5 PUT YOURSELF IN TIME-OUT

About eight days later Jesus took Peter, John, and James up on a mountain to pray. And as he was praying, the appearance of his face was transformed, and his clothes became dazzling white.

—Luke 9:28-29 NLT

Mountains, deserts, gardens, and seasides—four places Jesus frequently visited and took time out to spend in communion with the Father. What happened during those times? Jesus was transformed. While the transformation did not always reveal the full glory of Christ as on the mount of transfiguration, each time of communion and communication with the Father allowed the Spirit to rejuvenate, replenish, and direct the Son. This is how He was able to rule in life.

Though Jesus is the Son of God, maintaining oneness with the Father was His top priority on the earth. By spending time with Him, He stayed empowered by grace and submitted to the will of the Father.

What specifically can you do to increase your time in God's presence?

_____

_____

_____

_____

_____

Carefully read each passage and identify what happened after Jesus' time with the Father. What significant role do you think these times played in the miraculous outcomes?

Mark 6:45-51 _____

_____

Luke 6:12-16 _____

_____

Matthew 26:36-46, Luke 22:39-54; Matthew 14:22-36, Mark 6:45-56

_____

_____

_____

For Further Study...
Mark 1:35, 6:31-32;
Luke 5:16; John 18:1-2

Day 6 THE BEST IS YET TO COME!

I tell you the truth, anyone who believes in me will do the same works I have done, and even greater works, because I am going to be with the Father. You can ask for anything in my name, and I will do it, so that the Son can bring glory to the Father. Yes, ask me for anything in my name, and I will do it!

—John 14:12-14 NLT

Jesus ruled in life when He lived on earth. He was the exact likeness of the Father in heaven, and He only did what He saw the Father do (see Hebrews 1:3; John 5:19). The gospels record over three dozen miraculous acts at the hands of Jesus, but "there are so many other things Jesus did. If they were all written down...I can't imagine a world big enough to hold such a library of books" (John 21:25 The Message). Here is a sampling of what Jesus did:

Jesus Ruled in Life by...	See It for Yourself
Taking authority over the weather, rebuking a storm of hurricane proportions	Matthew 8:23-27; Mark 4:35-41
Multiplying food to feed over 5,000 and then over 4,000	Matthew 14:13-21;15:32-38; Mark 6:35-44; Luke 9:12-17; John 6:5-13
Bringing dead people back to life	Mark 5:35-43; Luke 7:11-15; John 11:41-44

Jesus said **you** would do *greater works* than He did. Why does God want you to do great works?

_____

_____

Name some of the "greater works," or manifestations, of God's power you have witnessed firsthand. Have you ever been the instrument through whom God flowed? How have these experiences impacted your faith and the faith of those who witnessed them?

_____

_____

Carefully read John 6:28-29, 15:1-8, and 1 John 5:14-15. What can you change in your life to be positioned for greater works? How are you challenged by these verses?

_____

_____

SESSION SUMMARY

As a believer, God's unlimited supply of *grace* is available to you. Through grace, you are made God's child and empowered to rule in every area of life. Grace infuses you with the fullness of Christ—His divine nature. Through grace, you have authority over all the power of the enemy and the ability to go beyond your natural ability. Grace is received anytime, anywhere through humble prayer.

Notes

_____

_____

_____

_____

_____

_____

_____

_____

_____

_____

_____

_____

_____

_____

_____

_____

_____

_____

_____

_____

_____

_____

_____

_____

_____

_____

_____

_____

_____

_____

_____

_____

_____

_____

_____

(1) Adapted from *Noah Webster's First Edition of an American Dictionary of the English Language* (1828), Republished in facsimile edition by Foundation for American Christian Education (San Francisco, CA 2000). (2) Adapted from *The New Unger's Bible Dictionary*, Merrill F. Unger (Chicago, IL: Moody Press, 1988). (3) Adapted from *Thayer's Greek-English Lexicon of the New Testament*, Joseph H. Thayer (Grand Rapids, MI: Baker Book House Company, 1977) p. 666. (4) Adapted from *Strong's Exhaustive Concordance of the Bible*, James Strong, LL.D., S.T.D. (Nashville, TN: Thomas Nelson Publishers, 1990). (5) *Standing Firm, 365 Devotions to Strengthen Your Faith*, compiled by Patti M. Hummel (St. San Luis Obispo, CA: Parable) p. 360. (6) *The Matthew Henry Study Bible*, KJV; A. Kenneth Abraham, General Editor (World Bible Publishers, Inc., 1994) note appearing with John 1:16. (7) Oswald Chambers, *My Utmost for His Highest* (Uhrichsville, OH: Barbour Publishing, Inc., MCMXCVII) p. 178. (8) Rick Renner, *Sparkling Gems from the Greek* (Tulsa, OK: Teach All Nations, 2003) p. 55. (9) Ibid (adapted).

> *You are a chosen race, a royal priesthood, a dedicated nation, [God's] own purchased, special people, that you may set forth the wonderful deeds and display the virtues and perfections of Him Who called you out of darkness into His marvelous light.*

—1 Peter 2:9 AMP

Chapter

3

DISTINGUISHED

Please refer to session 3 of the teaching series, along with chapters 4 and 5 in the Relentless book.

1. What an extraordinary life Jesus lived! Scripture says God's grace was upon Him, empowering Him to walk distinguished in every area of life. Name three ways in which Jesus lived distinguished. Of the three, which is the most challenging for you? Why?

3 ways Jesus lived a distinguished life:

1. _____

2. _____

3. _____

The most challenging for me is...

_____
_____
_____

G 2. If we try to live a holy life in our own ability, one of two mind-sets tends to develop: We either become *hypocritical legalists* (talking one way but living a different way) or we continue our loose lifestyle while holding firm to the unbiblical belief that "grace covers all the sin I've chosen to continue practicing." Do you find yourself leaning toward either of these mind-sets? If so, how is this session bringing you freedom?

_____

SETTING *the* PACE

"The key to *grace living* is not more self-effort and trying harder but getting closer to Christ. That's where the power is. ...Jesus Christ wants to express His life through you and be your *respirator*. You can't breathe spiritually without Him, and neither can I. His grace is the very oxygen in our lungs that makes the spiritual life possible. As we yield ourselves to Christ, He fills us with the incredible, life-giving gift of grace."
—*Tony Evans*[1]

CORE STRENGTHENER

Holiness is not a work of our flesh—it is a product of God's grace. Grace is God's empowering presence in our lives that gives us the ability to do what we otherwise couldn't do in our own ability. It enables us to cleanse ourselves of everything that makes our body and soul unclean and to live completely holy. This is the acceptable way to serve God.

---

*Therefore, since we are receiving a kingdom which cannot be shaken, **let us have grace**, by which we may serve God acceptably with reverence and godly fear.*
—Hebrews 12:28 NKJV

3. If we attempt to *earn* God's grace by being
[G] "good enough" or achieving worthy goals, we reduce grace to a load of our works. Read through the list of activities below. Have you ever attempted to earn God's grace through any of these?

Reading a certain amount of Scripture
Praying for a long time
Fasting
Being patient/kind with others
Serving in ministry
Helping the poor
Giving tithes and offerings
Sharing the Gospel
Going to church
Not committing a particular sin
Saying the right thing
Other _____

What has held you back from a greater understanding of God's free gift of grace?

_____
_____
_____
_____

Surrender any obstacle you struggle with to God in prayer. Keep in mind that grace is God's empowerment. It's the source of all His blessings, including wisdom, direction, creativity, anointing, and miraculous power. You cannot earn God's grace for any of these things. You must receive grace by faith with a humble heart.

G 4. By God's grace, Jesus also met the practical needs of mankind. He healed the sick, gave sight to the blind, opened deaf ears, made the lame to walk, multiplied food to feed the hungry, brought deliverance to the demon possessed, and even raised the dead. Carefully read these verses.

> And Jesus summoned to Him His twelve disciples and gave them power and authority over unclean spirits, to drive them out, and to cure all kinds of disease and all kinds of weakness and infirmity.
>
> —*Matthew 10:1 AMP*

> "These are the miraculous signs that will accompany believers: They will use the power and authority of my name to force demons out of people. They will speak new languages. They will pick up snakes, and if they drink any deadly poison, it will not hurt them. They will place their hands on the sick and cure them."
>
> —*Mark 16:17-18 GW*

> The apostles worked many miracles and wonders among the people. ...Many men and women started having faith in the Lord. Then sick people were brought out to the road and placed on cots and mats. It was hoped that Peter would walk by, and his shadow would fall on them and heal them. A lot of people living in the towns near Jerusalem brought those who were sick or troubled by evil spirits, and they were all healed.
>
> —*Acts 5:12, 14-16 CEV*

> God did extraordinary miracles through Paul, so that even handkerchiefs and aprons that had touched him were taken to the sick, and their illnesses were cured and the evil spirits left them.
>
> —*Acts 19:11-12 NIV*

What is the Lord showing you in these passages? What can *you* do as part of Christ to meet the needs of others?

_____

_____

_____

_____

Group leader extras: Luke 4:38-41; Acts 28:1-6.

> *Most certainly and thoroughly I now perceive and understand that God shows no partiality and is* **no respecter of persons***.*
> —Acts 10:34 AMP

CORE STRENGTHENER

The grace of God on Jesus' life gave Him the ability to change the societies He was a part of. Now He charges us, "As the Father has sent Me, I also send you" (John 20:21 NKJV). We are to change our societies as Jesus changed His: through the free gift of God's grace!

5. Do you need wisdom? The fullness of God's grace provides it. **Meditate on the message** of these scriptures. What is the Lord speaking to you about receiving wisdom, insight, and understanding? What difficult situation do you need answers for right now? Stop and pray for God's insight or creative solution. Write what He speaks to you.

> Yes, if you want better insight and discernment, and are searching for them as you would for lost money or hidden treasure, then wisdom will be given you, and knowledge of God himself; you will soon learn the importance of reverence for the Lord and of trusting him. For the Lord grants wisdom! His every word is a treasure of knowledge and understanding. He grants good sense to the godly—his saints. He is their shield, protecting them and guarding their pathway. He shows how to distinguish right from wrong, how to find the right decision every time. For wisdom and truth will enter the very center of your being, filling your life with joy.
>
> —Proverbs 2:3-10 TLB

> God has hidden all the treasures of wisdom and knowledge in Christ.
>
> —Colossians 2:3 GW

> If you need wisdom—if you want to know what God wants you to do—ask him, and he will gladly tell you. He will not resent your asking. But when you ask him, be sure that you really expect him to answer.
>
> —James 1:5-6 NLT

The difficult situation I am facing is...

_____

_____

_____

Group leader extras: Daniel 2:21; Matthew 7:24; Luke 21:15; John 8:31-32.

The insight or creative solution God is showing me is...

_____

_____

_____

_____

The wisdom of God for your situation may not come today, but it will come. When you've received insight from God, take time to write it down and thank Him.

DISTINGUISHED

"Separated or known by a mark of difference or different qualities; separated from others by superior or extraordinary qualities." A person can be distinguished in demeanor and behavior as well as in their attitude and actions. Interestingly, the primary root of the word *distinguish* means "to prick or pierce with a sharp point; the practice of making marks by puncturing." This root is where we get the verb *to stick*.[3] Applying this definition to ourselves, we must ask: *Are we living in such a way that we're pricking or piercing the lives of others to want to turn toward God?*

SETTING *the* PACE

"**Wisdom** is the capacity to see things from God's viewpoint. ...Never lose sight of the fact that God sees the totality of your life. He knows you inside and out. He knows your thoughts, your feelings, your physical makeup. He knows your past, your present, and your future. He knows your natural talents, your experiences, your spiritual gifts. God sees the whole of who you are, what you are called to do, and what you are facing right now. The more you see your life from God's perspective, the stronger your ability to discern the right way to go."
—*Charles Stanley*[2]

G 6. To be **distinguished** means to live a stand-out, extraordinary life that leaves an indelible mark on others. Slowly read the verses below and identify the positive impact of a distinguished life. In what practical ways can you encourage and motivate your friends and family to live distinguished?

Let your light so shine before men that they may see your moral excellence and your praiseworthy, noble, and good deeds and recognize and honor and praise and glorify your Father Who is in heaven.

—*Matthew 5:16 AMP*

Live an exemplary life among the natives so that your actions will refute their prejudices. Then they'll be won over to God's side and be there to join in the celebration when he arrives.

—*1 Peter 2:12 The Message*

Always set an example by doing good things. When you teach, be an example of moral purity and dignity. Speak an accurate message that cannot be condemned. Then those who oppose us will be ashamed because they cannot say anything bad about us. Urge slaves [*employees*] to obey their masters and to try their best to satisfy them. They must not talk back, nor steal, but must show themselves to be entirely trustworthy. In this way they will make people want to believe in our Savior and God.

—*Titus 2:7-8 GW 9-10 TLB*
[Italicized words in brackets added for clarity.]

The positive impact of a distinguished life includes...

_____

_____

_____

Ways I can encourage others to live a distinguished life include...

_____

_____

_____

Let us think of ways to motivate one another to acts of love and good works.
—Hebrews 10:24 NLT

Character Profile
DANIEL

Lifespan: Approximately 620 B.C to 535 B.C.
Occupation: Prophet and government official
Place of Service: Courts of Babylon and Medo-Persia
Contemporaries: Ezekiel, Jeremiah, and Habakkuk
Words Describing Daniel: Dedicated, committed, uncompromising, distinguished, excellent, trustworthy, relentless

Daniel, whose name means "God is my judge," was raised with the rich heritage of the Jewish nobility (see Daniel 1:3). In 605 B.C., when he was about 15 or 16, the Babylonian king Nebuchadnezzar laid siege to Jerusalem, and Daniel was deported to Babylon. After a three-year education in the Babylonian tradition (see Daniel 1:4-5), he went on to serve at least four Gentile kings: Nebuchadnezzar and Belshazzar of Babylon and Darius and Cyrus of the Medo-Persians.

Daniel's life was *not* what he had planned. Nevertheless, he remained faithful to God and brought Him great glory for nearly 70 years. He is the only known prophet to serve exclusively in foreign lands. Simultaneously functioning in ministry and politics, he became an evangelist to his enemy captors. He was hated by the Babylonian and Medo-Persian wise men, unjustly treated, and thrown into a den of lions in his old age. But God was faithful to rescue him and give him divine wisdom, insight into the future, and the ability to interpret dreams. Daniel never gave up and never gave in. He was relentless in his walk with God and highly distinguished among men.[4]

What can you learn from Daniel? Read his book for yourself. Learn how he distinguished himself and remained godly in an ungodly world.

---

*This man, Daniel, **distinguished himself** among the other officials
and satraps because there was an extraordinary spirit in him.*
—Daniel 6:3 GW

G 7. Stop and ask yourself, *Am I distinguishing myself as Daniel did? Am I allowing God's extraordinary Spirit to fully live through me? How is God's grace distinguishing my level of wisdom, productivity, creativity, etc.? Where can I distinguish myself more?* Pray and ask God for His input. Write what He reveals.

God's grace is distinguishing me in the areas of...

_____

_____

_____

Areas where I can distinguish myself more are...

_____

_____

_____

Group leader extra: Encourage students to ask others who know and love them these questions. A friend's perspective can often help us see things we would otherwise miss (see Proverbs 27:17).

8. Is there an area in your life where you feel unqualified but you sense God is calling you to distinguish yourself? What is it and how does this session encourage you to believe and receive God's grace to empower you?

_____

_____

_____

G 9. Were you a part of the 98 percent of Christians who do *not* understand God's grace is His empowerment? What part(s) of the teaching exploded in your heart and helped you see grace in a greater way? What action(s) is the Holy Spirit prompting you to take?

The *truths* that helped me see grace in a greater way are...

CORE STRENGTHENER

You are not who you are because of who you were born to, or what side of the tracks you grew up on, or what ethnic group you belong to, or where you were schooled. **You are who you are by the grace of God!**

_____

_____

_____

The *actions* the Holy Spirit is prompting me to take is...

_____

_____

_____

10. Take a few moments to recall the core principles of this week's session. Then, in your own words, briefly describe how God's grace empowers you to live a distinguished life.

Grace enables me to live a distinguished life by...

_____

_____

_____

Do you know someone who would be strengthened by this truth? Take time to share it with them.

For more on this topic, see John's* Extraordinary *curriculum.

SETTING *the* PACE

"Almighty God, who created us in your image: **Grant us grace** fearlessly to contend against evil and to make no peace with oppression; and, that we may reverently use our freedom, help us to employ it in the maintenance of justice in our communities and among the nations, to the glory of your holy Name."
—*William Wilberforce*[5]

Weekly CHALLENGE

Find a need you can meet. Perhaps someone around you is in financial trouble and you can help them pay a bill or buy groceries. You can volunteer to babysit for a single mother so she can enjoy some time to herself. You can invite single college students to your home for dinner and a game night. Ask the Holy Spirit to open your eyes to a need in your world and show you how you can respond to it.

Day 1 **GROW IN GRACE**

*But **grow in grace** (undeserved favor, spiritual strength) and recognition and knowledge and understanding of our Lord and Savior Jesus Christ (the Messiah). To Him [be] glory (honor, majesty, and splendor) both now and to the day of eternity. Amen (so be it)!*

—2 Peter 3:18 AMP

Grace is God's empowerment for living. Like the breath in our lungs and the blood in our veins, it brings life to every aspect of who we are. God instructs us through the apostle Peter to grow in grace. The word grow indicates time, and time indicates process. Indeed, growing in grace is a *lifetime process* overseen by God and carried out by the Holy Spirit.

Growing in grace is maturing in Christ. This manner of living is what God has ordained for all of His children (see Romans 8:29-30). It is what Paul referred to when he said we grow from "faith to faith" and "glory to glory" (see Romans 1:17; 2 Corinthians 3:18). Step by step, day by day we learn how to ask for, receive, and employ God's grace. Look at what Paul says:

And now [brethren], I commit you to God [I deposit you in His charge, entrusting you to His protection and care]. And I commend you to the **Word of His grace** [to the commands and counsels and promises of His unmerited favor]. It is able to build you up and to give you [your rightful] inheritance among all God's set-apart ones (those consecrated, purified, and transformed of soul).

—*Acts 20:32 AMP*

What is the source of grace? What does it do, and what can you do to ensure you grow in it?

According to Ephesians 4:11-16, what else has the Lord provided to help you grow spiritually? What does this passage speak to you?

Read Hebrews 12:14-15. What is the connection between these two verses, and what does it have to do with *failing to secure* or *missing out on* the grace of God?

Related scriptures: Ephesians 4:30-32; 1 Corinthians 1:10.

SETTING *the* PACE

"Our New Testament contains 155 references to grace; 130 of them come from the pen of Paul. The word opens, closes, and dominates every letter he wrote. It defines his teaching and his dearest hopes. Grace is the magnificent ideal by which he would measure his life and yours."

—*David Jeremiah*[6]

Day 2 GRACE ENABLES YOU TO BE PURE

*We beg you who have received God's grace not to let it be wasted...so then, **let us purify ourselves** from everything that makes body or soul unclean, and let us be completely holy.*

—2 Corinthians 6:1; 7:1 TEV

One major blessing of God's empowering grace is the ability to live a pure, holy life just like Jesus did. While His blood cleanses us of all sin, we are called upon to cooperate with the Holy Spirit and purify our lives of things that defile our body and soul (our *mind, will,* and *emotions*). This includes attitudes and actions that are not in agreement with God's Word. How do we do it? By God's grace. Grace is wasted if we don't use it to purify ourselves.

What kinds of things does God consider *unclean* or *impure*?
Read Ephesians 5:3-5 • James 1:19-21; 3:5-10 • 1 Peter 2:1 • 2 Corinthians 6:14-7:1

_____

_____

Read Matthew 15:10 11, 18. Where do impurities come from? How can you guard against them?

_____

_____

What has God given us to purify ourselves? How do we make use of it?
Read Psalm 119:9, 11 • John 15:3, 17:17 • Ephesians 5:25-26 • James 1:21-25 • 1 Peter 1:22, 2:2 • Colossians 3:16

_____

_____

Who else plays a part in the purifying process? How are we to respond?
Read Philippians 1:6; 2:12-13 • 1 Thessalonians 5:23-24 • Romans 6:19, 22

_____

_____

Is the Holy Spirit showing you anything unclean in your life? It may be an attitude, activity, relationship, or way of thinking or speaking. How can you cooperate with Him and purify yourself?

_____

_____

_____

_____

For Further Study...
Isaiah 1:16; Jeremiah 4:14; James 4:8; 1 John 3:3; 2 Timothy 2:20-23

Day 3 GRACE ENABLES YOU TO SHINE BRIGHTLY

Arise, my people! Let your light shine for all the nations to see! For the glory of the Lord is streaming from you. Darkness as black as night shall cover all the peoples of the earth, but the glory of the Lord will shine from you. All nations will come to your light; mighty kings will come to see the glory of the Lord upon you.
—Isaiah 60:1-3 TLB

"God said, 'I command light to shine!' And light started shining." (Genesis 1:3 CEV) That was His desire in the beginning, and it's still His desire today. Jesus said,

"You're here to be light, bringing out the God-colors in the world. God is not a secret to be kept. We're going public with this, as public as a city on a hill. If I make you light-bearers, you don't think I'm going to hide you under a bucket, do you? I'm putting you on a light stand. Now that I've put you there on a hilltop, on a light stand—**shine!** Keep open house; be generous with your lives. By opening up to others, you'll prompt people to open up with God, this generous Father in heaven."
—Matthew 5:14-16 The Message

Consider these words from Jesus and God's clarion call in Isaiah 60:1-3. What is the Lord saying to you about being His light?

_____

_____

Imagine it's the dead of winter and a major power outage hits and lasts for several days. Nights are long, and it is too dark to see your hand in front of your face. Think of the joy you feel when light returns. How does this help you have greater compassion for those in spiritual darkness? How will it change the way you act at the store, in your neighborhood, with your family, etc.?

_____

_____

_____

What causes God's glory to shine forth in us?
Read Psalm 34:5 • 2 Corinthians 3:18, 4:6 • Philippians 2:14-15 • Isaiah 58:10

_____

_____

Related Scriptures: Ecclesiastes 8:1; Psalm 19:8; 119:105, 130; 2 Peter 1:19.

CORE STRENGTHENER

Each of us is called to different sectors of society. Wherever we're located in life's arena, we should manifest headship and leadership. Our creativity should inspire and be sought after on every level. When believers are involved, there should be an abundance of creativity, productivity, tranquility, sensitivity, and ingenuity. Through God's grace, we are to be light in a dark world.

Day 4 YOU ARE DESIGNED FOR A PURPOSE!

Each person is given something to do that shows who God is: Everyone gets in on it, everyone benefits.

—1 Corinthians 12:7 The Message

Your fingerprints and voice patterns, the design of your eyes, and the dental impressions of your teeth—all say one thing: you are one-of-a-kind. God has also given you gifts, talents, and abilities that set you apart. You are equipped to carry out a particular mission that no one else on Earth has been assigned. God and others are counting on you to come through.

Believe it or not, every day of your life was written down *before* you were born! Before there were social media networks to update—before the earth's foundation—God had a play-by-play of your every day recorded. Look at what He says in His Word:

You made all the delicate, inner parts of my body and knit me together in my mother's womb. Thank you for making me so wonderfully complex! Your workmanship is marvelous—how well I know it. You watched me as I was being formed in utter seclusion, as I was woven together in the dark of the womb. You saw me before I was born. Every day of my life was recorded in your book. Every moment was laid out before a single day had passed. How precious are your thoughts about me, O God. They cannot be numbered! I can't even count them; they outnumber the grains of sand.

—Psalm 139:13-18 NLT

Do you believe God is mindful of you and has a good plan for your life? Do you believe that His thoughts about you are precious and uncountable? What is He speaking to you in these verses?

_____

_____

Identify your gifts and talents. What are you really good at? What do others say you're good at? What do you enjoy doing? Can you see a connection? These answers help give you a snapshot of your calling.

I enjoy or excel in:

_____

Other people say I am good at:

_____

In light of these answers, I feel my calling in life is:

_____

_____

For Further Study...
Jeremiah 1:5; Isaiah 49:1; Ephesians 2:10; Jeremiah 29:11; Romans 12:4-8

Day 5 YOU ARE STRATEGICALLY PLACED

Therefore, whenever we have the opportunity, we should do good to everyone—especially to those in the family of faith.

—Galatians 6:10 NLT

God has His people everywhere. Where you are is no accident—you are strategically placed. His purpose is for you to rule in life right where you are, to tangibly manifest the qualities of His Kingdom and bring Him glory. As part of Christ, you're empowered to promote good, extinguish evil, and offer hope in marvelous ways.

Why does God give us grace? Why does He give us anointing, wisdom, creativity, and the resurrection power of His Spirit? It is not just to benefit ourselves and our families. He's given us the empowerment of His grace to be a storehouse of provision for those around us—the people we are connected to already and those we come into contact with in our sphere of influence.

Look back over your life. Who has God used to be a blessing to you? Where might you be if they hadn't?

_____

_____

Are you a *reservoir* that just takes blessings in or a pipe through which God can flow?

_____

Pray and ask God to give you a heart that is sensitive and desires to help others.

Who are you presently pouring into in your sphere of influence? Is there an individual, family, community, or group you feel God wants you to aid? How?

_____

_____

God wants us to be especially mindful of *widows, orphans* and the *poor. Read* Psalm 68:5; 146:5-9 • Proverbs 15:25 • Jeremiah 49:11 • James 1:27

What does God want us to do for them? How will we be blessed?
Read Psalm 41:1-3, 82:3-4 • Isaiah 1:17 • Jeremiah 22:3 • Proverbs 19:17, 21:13, 28:27

_____

_____

What family, individual, or organization will you support to fulfill this commission?

_____

_____

Day 6 YOU ARE DESTINED TO WIN!

*The LORD will make you the **head**, not the tail. You will always be at the top, never at the bottom, if you faithfully obey the commands of the LORD your God that I am giving you today.*

—Deuteronomy 28:13 GW

To rule in life by the grace of God means to break free from the status quo. Your existence is not about getting a paycheck every other week, building up money in the bank, and retiring some day. You have become a leader and trendsetter in your sphere of influence. You are bringing heaven to earth!

In what field of influence do you regularly function?

Examples: Medicine, education, politics, construction, media, customer service, business, ministry, parenting, etc.

Describe what *ruling in life* in **your** work looks like. How should others be responding?

The one condition God placed upon making us the "head" is to *obey His commands*. Read the story of Saul's downfall in 1 Samuel 15. What can you learn from Saul's example and apply in your own life? What is obedience in God's eyes?

Obedience brings blessings! Identify the promises in these scriptures.
Matthew 12:50 • John 14:23, 15:9-11 • Deuteronomy 28:1-14 • Joshua 1:7-8 • 1 Kings 3:14 • Isaiah 1:19

Get quiet before the Lord. Ask Him if there is anything He has asked you to do that you have done partially or not at all. Write what He reveals. If necessary, ask Him to forgive you for disobeying and to give you the grace to obey His direction completely.

SESSION SUMMARY
Grace is God's empowerment to live a distinguished life like Jesus did. Wisdom, creativity, purity, holiness, and the ability to change society are all possible through grace. Wherever you go and whatever you do, God wants you to shine forth His character and bring Him glory.

Notes

_____

_____

_____

_____

_____

_____

_____

_____

_____

_____

_____

_____

_____

_____

_____

_____

_____

_____

_____

_____

_____

_____

_____

_____

_____

_____

_____

_____

_____

_____

_____

_____

_____

(1) Tony Evans, *Free at Last* (Chicago, IL: Moody Publications, 2001) pp. 97, 99. (2) Charles Stanley, *Walking Wisely* (Nashville, TN: Thomas Nelson Publishers, 2002) pp. 18, 42. (3) Adapted from *Noah Webster's First Edition of an American Dictionary of the English Language* (1828), Republished in facsimile edition by Foundation for American Christian Education (San Francisco, CA 2000). (4) Adapted from: the *Life Application Bible copyright* © 1988, 1989, 1990, 1991 Tyndale House Publishers, Inc. Wheaton, IL 60189. All Rights reserved. (New International Version edition, pp. 1473-1475). New International Version edition is published jointly by Tyndale House Publishers, Inc. and Zondervan Publishing House. Also adapted from *The Word In Life™ Study Bible* copyright © 1993, 1996 by Thomas Nelson, Inc. Used by Permission (New King James Version, pp. 1444-1452). (5) *Standing Firm, 365 Devotions to Strengthen Your Faith*, compiled by Patti M. Hummel (St. San Luis Obispo, CA: Parable) p. 226. (6) David Jeremiah, *Captured by Grace* (Nashville, TN: Thomas Nelson, Inc., 2006) p. 13.

*Jesus replied, "I assure you, unless you are born again, you can never **see** the Kingdom of God. ...The truth is, no one can **enter** the Kingdom of God without being born of water and the Spirit."*

—John 3:3, 5 NLT

4

SEE OR ENTER

Please refer to session 4 of the teaching series, along with chapter 6 in the Relentless book.

CORE STRENGTHENER

1. If you want to rule in life, then you must understand the Kingdom of God. Consider these words from Jesus and the apostle Paul. Where is the Kingdom of God and what kinds of things does it consist of? What is it *not*?

> Asked by the Pharisees when the kingdom of God would come, He replied to them by saying, The kingdom of God does not come with signs to be observed or with visible display, nor will people say, Look! Here [it is]! or, See, [it is] there! For behold, the kingdom of God is within you [in your hearts] and among you [surrounding you].
>
> *—Luke 17:20-21 AMP*

> God's kingdom isn't about eating and drinking. It is about pleasing God, about living in peace, and about true happiness. All this comes from the Holy Spirit.
>
> *—Romans 14:17 CEV*

Jesus talks a lot about the Kingdom of God. In fact, it is mentioned over 100 times in the New Testament. Many people see the Kingdom of God as heaven; but in reality, when Jesus talks about the Kingdom, He is talking about **the rule of God**. All who have received God's grace and are freely put right with Him are to rule in life—we are to advance His Kingdom, bringing His way of life to the earth.

> For the Kingdom of God is not just a lot of talk; it is living by God's power.
>
> *—1 Corinthians 4:20 NLT*

Group leader extra: John 18:36

KINGDOM OF GOD

The Greek words most frequently used in the New Testament for the *Kingdom of God* are *basileia tou Theos*. *Theos* means "God, the supreme

Deity," and *basileia* refers to "royalty, rule, or realm of reign," and is taken from the root word meaning "foundation of power."[1] So it could be said that the Kingdom of God is *God's royal rule* or *God's imperial rule*. One definition of the word *imperial* is "supremely powerful." Therefore, the Kingdom of God is **God's supreme, powerful rule.**[2]

Life Lessons from God's Kingdom

The Kingdom of God is like...	Life Lesson	Find it
A king who wanted to settle accounts with his servants	Forgiveness	Matthew 18:21-35
A farmer who scattered seed on the ground	God brings the increase	Mark 4:26-29
A mustard seed	Never underestimate the power of God	Matthew 13:31-32; Mark 4:30-32; Luke 13:18-19
A man who planted good seed in his field	There are true and false believers; God will judge who is who	Matthew 13:24-30, 36-43
Leaven that a woman placed in a huge amount of dough	God's power has potent, far-reaching effects	Matthew 13:33; Luke 13:20-21
Treasure a man found hidden in a field	The value of God's Kingdom is incomparable	Matthew 13:44
A merchant who was searching for fine pearls	The value of God's Kingdom is incomparable	Matthew 13:45-46
A fishing net thrown in the sea that gathers fish of every kind	God is the ultimate Judge	Matthew 13:47-50
A homeowner who brings out new and old treasures	Jesus' "new" teaching is connected to and supported by the Old Testament	Matthew 13:52
A landowner who hired workers for his vineyard	All are saved by grace	Matthew 20:1-16
A king who gave a great banquet	God earnestly wants everyone to be with Him in heaven	Matthew 22:1-14; Luke 14:15-24
Ten virgins who took their lamps to go meet the groom	Be ready at all times for Christ's return	Matthew 25:1-13
An employer who gave talents to his servants to invest	God gives each of us the gifts He knows we can handle and expects a return	Matthew 25:14-30

2. When you see *the Kingdom of God* in Scripture, substitute the phrase with its original Greek meaning: **God's supreme, powerful rule.** This gives us a much clearer, more relevant meaning. Pause and ponder these amazing declarations.

Our Father in heaven, hallowed be Your name. Your [*supreme, powerful rule*] come. Your will be done on earth as it is in heaven.

—*Luke 11:2 NKJV*

God blesses you who are poor, for [*God's supreme, powerful rule*] is yours.

—*Luke 6:20 NLT*

When Jesus saw what was happening, he was angry with his disciples. He said to them, "Let the children come to me. Don't stop them! For [*God's supreme, powerful rule*] belongs to those who are like these children. I tell you the truth, anyone who doesn't receive [*God's supreme, powerful rule*] like a child will never enter it."

—*Mark 10:14-15 NLT*

Seek [*God's supreme, powerful rule*] above all else, and he will give you everything you need.

—*Luke 12:31 NLT*

What is the Lord showing you about the Kingdom of God—His supreme, powerful rule?

----

*Jesus replied, "I assure you, unless you are born again, you can never **see** the Kingdom of God. ...The truth is, no one can **enter** the Kingdom of God without being born of water and the Spirit."*
—John 3:3, 5 NLT

3. Believers who simply *see* the Kingdom of God are like *passengers* in an airplane. Believers who *enter* the Kingdom are like *pilots*. Describe the difference between being a "passenger" and "pilot" Christian. What advantages do pilots have? Which one are you?

SETTING *the* PACE

"'*Your kingdom come. Your will be done on earth as it is in heaven.*' This statement simply means that a true person of prayer is not interested in his own kingdom. His interest is in God's kingdom and what He wants accomplished. ...We are to ask, 'Father, what do *You* want done? What do *You* want to happen on earth?' God is delighted when you are excited about the things He's excited about. He will bless you in the course of accomplishing His work on earth."

—*Dr. Myles Munroe*[3]

Passenger Christians   Pilot Christians

_____   _____
_____   _____
_____   _____
_____   _____
_____   _____
_____

SEE or ENTER

The original Greek word for **see** in John 3:3 is *eido*, which means "to literally see" or "to know, be acquainted with or be aware of." In John 3:5, Jesus takes believers to a new level using the word **enter**—the Greek word *eiserchomai*, which means "to arise and come into" or "enter in."[4] All of God's children are able to *see* the Kingdom—they are acquainted with and aware of God's supreme, powerful rule. But not all of His children *enter* the Kingdom. Those who **enter** actually *arise and come into* God's supreme, powerful rule. There is a big difference.

G 4. Jesus says it's virtually impossible for someone *rich* to enter the Kingdom—God's supreme, powerful rule (see Matthew 19:24). But to those who are *poor*, the Kingdom is freely given (see Luke 6:20). Explain what Jesus means by *rich* and *poor*. What mind-set does each have and on what are they relying?

Those who are RICH are...

_____
_____
_____
_____

Those who are POOR are...

_____
_____
_____
_____

Group extra: See page 65 in *Relentless*.

5. In order for us to move from *seeing* the Kingdom to actually *entering* it, we must pass through many *tribulations* (see Acts 14:22). But God doesn't want us to get down—He wants us to cheer up!

Meditate on the message of these powerful promises...

I have told you these things, so that in Me you may have [perfect] peace and confidence. In the world you have tribulation and trials and distress and frustration; but be of good cheer [take courage; be confident, certain, undaunted]! For I have overcome the world. **[I have deprived it of power to harm you and have conquered it for you.]**

—John 16:33 AMP

Do not be afraid, for I have ransomed you. I have called you by name; you are mine. When you go through deep waters, I will be with you. When you go through rivers of difficulty, you will not drown. When you walk through the fire of oppression, you will not be burned up; the flames will not consume you. For I am the Lord, your God, the Holy One of Israel, your Savior.

—Isaiah 43:1-3 NLT

For He [God] Himself has said, I will not in any way fail you nor give you up nor leave you without support. [I will] not, [I will] not, [I will] not in any degree leave you helpless nor forsake nor let [you] down (relax My hold on you)! [Assuredly not!] So we take comfort and are encouraged and confidently and boldly say, The Lord is my Helper; I will not be seized with alarm [I will not fear or dread or be terrified]. What can man do to me?

—Hebrews 13:5-6 AMP

How do these promises from God encourage and strengthen you to face life's trials?

_____

_____

_____

_____

Group leader extras: Psalm 28:6-9; 37:23-24, 39-40; Proverbs 2:8; Isaiah 41:10-14, 54:10; 2 Timothy 4:18.

TRIBULATION

The original Greek word for tribulation is *thlipsis*. James Strong defines it as "pressure, persecution, affliction, or trouble."[5] Thayer's Lexicon describes it as "the pressure or distress of a woman in childbirth."[6] *The Encyclopedia of Biblical Words* states *thlipsis* is "the idea of great emotional and spiritual stress that can be caused by external or internal pressures. Of the fifty-five uses of this root in the New Testament, fifty-three are figurative. The pressure may come from enemies, adverse circumstances, wrong decisions, or passion run awry."[7]

SETTING *the* PACE

"If our Father permits a trial to come, it must be because that trial is the sweetest and best thing that could happen to us, and we must accept it with thanks from His dear hand. The trial itself may be hard to flesh and blood, and I do not mean that we can like or enjoy the suffering of it. But we can and must love the will of God in the trial, for His will is always sweet, whether it is in joy or in sorrow. Our trials may be our chariots...to bear us to the longed-for triumph."
—*Hannah Whitall Smith*[8]

6. We are going to have tribulations, but God will never lead us into a storm He doesn't give us the power to overcome. Describe a storm you are presently in. Knowing what Jesus experienced, what can you expect to happen once you successfully come through this storm?

Meditate on the message of these verses for insight.

Then Jesus returned {*from the wilderness*} in the power of the Spirit to Galilee, and news of Him went out through all the surrounding region.

—*Luke 4:14 NKJV*

For I consider that the sufferings of this present time (this present life) are not worth being compared with the glory that is about to be revealed to us and in us and for us and conferred on us!

—*Romans 8:18 AMP*

Blessed is the man who perseveres under trial, because when he has stood the test, he will receive the crown of life that God has promised to those who love him.

—*James 1:12 NIV*

And after you have suffered a little while, the God of all grace [Who imparts all blessing and favor], Who has called you to His [own] eternal glory in Christ Jesus, will Himself complete and make you what you ought to be, establish and ground you securely, and strengthen, and settle you.

—*1 Peter 5:10 AMP*
{Italicized words in brackets added for clarity.}

The storm I'm in...

_____

_____

_____

Based on God's Word, I expect...

_____

Group leader extra: See pages 72-74 in Relentless.

G 7. Tribulation produces suffering, but if we suffer with Jesus, we will also be glorified with Him and share in His resurrection power. In your own words, briefly explain the two types of suffering: one for the world's sake and one for righteousness. In what area of your life will you or do you suffer for righteousness?

Suffering for the *world's sake*

_____

_____

_____

_____

Suffering for *righteousness*

_____

SETTING *the* PACE

"Paul uses the Greek word *thlipsis* for 'suffering,' and the idea is a kind of pressure, as in squeezing grapes to extract the juice. We don't go looking for trouble, but we certainly do make use of it. Bad times are our fuel for transformation. They make us stronger, nobler, wiser, and more worthy of serving God in ever-increasing capacity."

—David Jeremiah[9]

CORE STRENGTHENER

I will praise and give thanks to You with uprightness of heart when I learn [by sanctified experiences] Your righteous judgments [Your decisions against and punishments for particular lines of thought and conduct].
—Psalm 119:7 AMP

God does **not** author tribulation (*thlipsis*). He knows we live in a world contrary to His ways, and if we are going to be conquerors and rule in life, we are going to encounter resistance from evil forces. Therefore, He trains us in areas He knows we can handle in order to strengthen us for greater conquests.

8. Every trouble is a *sanctified experience* in the hand of God. If handled correctly by His grace, it will strengthen us to rule in life in greater ways than we dreamed. Think back to a major trial—one that was long and intense—you experienced and came through. How did it make you more like Christ and empower you to minister to others better?

_____

_____

_____

The Lord will deliver me from every evil attack and will bring me safely into his heavenly Kingdom. All glory to God forever and ever! Amen.
—2 Timothy 4:18 NLT

G 9. Getting God's perspective on tribulation and suffering is vitally important. As this session ends, how do you see hardship more clearly? What is the most encouraging truth you have learned? Take time to thank God and share with others what you have learned.

_____

_____

_____

SETTING *the* PACE

"Suffering will never be completely absent from our lives. So don't be afraid of suffering. Your suffering is a great means of love, If you make use of it. ...Suffering in and of itself is useless, but suffering that is shared with the passion of Christ is a wonderful gift and a sign of love. Christ's suffering proved to be a gift, the greatest gift of love, because through his suffering our sins were atoned for."
—Mother Teresa[10]

Weekly CHALLENGE

This week, make time to read one or more of the Gospels, substituting the phrase *God's supreme, powerful rule* wherever the *Kingdom of God* appears. Meditate on these verses and ask God to increase your revelation of His present-tense authority over and within you. Record what you learn below.

_____

_____

_____

_____

_____

_____

_____

_____

_____

_____

_____

_____

_____

_____

_____

_____

Day 1 **BE FILLED WITH THE HOLY SPIRIT**

Ever be filled and stimulated with the [Holy] Spirit.

—Ephesians 5:18 AMP

What a blessing is the Holy Spirit! He is the Spirit of Grace who gives us grace and enforces its power in our lives. On the day of Pentecost, He came to dwell in the spirit of man for the first time. This outpouring prophesied by Joel marked the beginning of the full force of God's Kingdom invading earth (see Joel 2:28-29).

In this new dimension of divine intervention, Jesus' followers were empowered to enter and advance God's supreme, powerful rule. What was true for the disciples then is true for us now. We will see God's Kingdom come "not by might nor by power, but by My Spirit, says the Lord of hosts!" (Zechariah 4:6 NKJV) This is why God wants us to be **full** of His Spirit every day.

If a glass is *full* of water, it has no room for anything else. If we're full of things other than God's Spirit, we will not have room for Him. Consider the thoughts that fill your mind, the requests that fill your prayers, and the activities that fill your days. What are you full of? Is it a mixture of things? Pray and ask God to reveal what's in your heart.

Read John 14:16-17, 26 and 16:12-15 and the believer's prayer in Acts 4:23-33. If you are full of the Holy Spirit, how can you expect His grace to manifest?

Read Isaiah 40:28-31, Acts 1:4-5, 8 and Psalm 23:1-3, 5. What principles can you identify and practice daily to stay full of God's Spirit?

For Further Study...
Ephesians 3:14-19;
Colossians 1:9-13

SETTING *the* PACE

"The grace of God that was given to the persecuting Saul is available for you. The same Holy Ghost infilling he received is likewise available. Do not rest satisfied with any lesser experience than the Baptism that the disciples received on the Day of Pentecost, then move on to a life of continuous receiving of more and more of the blessed Spirit of God."

—*Smith Wigglesworth*[11]

Day 2 SATURATE YOURSELF IN THE WORD

*Let Christ's **word** with all its wisdom and richness **live in you**. Use psalms, hymns, and spiritual songs to teach and instruct yourselves about God's kindness. Sing to God in your hearts.*

—Colossians 3:16 GW

One of the most valuable things you can do, especially in the midst of trouble, is to saturate yourself in God's Word. In the hands of the Holy Spirit, nothing packs more power. John's mother-in-law, Shirley, developed this practice when she was diagnosed with terminal cancer. She shut out every negative report and nagging thought of defeat and replaced it with the truth of Scripture. By relentlessly fighting the intense *thlipsis* with the Word, she received the crown of life and now rules in the area she persevered in. What a testimony of God's empowering grace!

Why is the Word more valuable than any other source of information known to man?
Read Psalm 119:89 • Isaiah 40:8 • Matthew 24:35 • 1 Peter 1:25 • 2 Timothy 3:16-17 • 2 Peter 1:20-21

How will its inherent *power* affect your life?
Read Hebrews 4:12 • James 1:21 • John 8:31-32 • Jeremiah 23:29 • Proverbs 4:20-22 • Psalm 19:7-11, 107:20

What is your *plan* of action to saturate yourself in God's Word? Pray and ask Him for a practical method to absorb the rich nutrients of His timeless truth. He knows the demands on your time and will show you what will work best. Write what He speaks to your heart.

Consider these tools: godly books, teachings, downloads, studies, and music

Day 3 CHOOSE YOUR FRIENDS WISELY

I choose as my friends everyone who worships you and follows your teachings.
—Psalm 119:63 CEV

Another life-changing habit you can cultivate is being mindful of who your closest friends are. The old saying is true: Show me your friends and I'll show you your future. Our *inner circle* of friends has a powerful impact on the direction and quality of our lives. While good companionship motivates us to do good and follow God with a greater intensity, bad company tends to stifle the life of Christ in us and may lead us in the wrong direction. If we are going to live relentlessly for Him, we must be wise about who we're spending a lot of time with.

Read Psalm 1:1 • Proverbs 4:14-15, 22:24-25, 24:1-2 • 1 Corinthians 5:11, 15:33 • 2 Corinthians 6:14-18 • Proverbs 13:20; 17:17; 27:5-6, 17 • Ecclesiastes 4:9-10 • Malachi 3:16-17

We are to reach out to the lost and influence those caught in compromise. How can you be selective about your inner circle of friends and still be salt and light to the unsaved or deceived?

_____

_____

You're here to be light, bringing out the God-colors in the world.
God is not a secret to be kept. We're going public with this,
as public as a city on a hill. ...I'm putting you on a light stand. Now that
*I've put you there on a hilltop, on a light stand—**shine**! Keep open house;*
be generous with your lives. By opening up to others, you'll prompt
people to open up with God, this generous Father in heaven.
—Matthew 5:14-16 The Message

Who in your life encourages you to follow God, believe His Word, and grow in Christ?

_____

_____

Thank God for these people, pray for them, and look for opportunities to fellowship with them more.

Take time to describe traits of "the perfect friend." How would they help you live relentlessly? What would they say and do? Ask God for grace to *be* this kind of friend to others. How can you be this friend to those in your sphere of influence?

_____

_____

_____

Day 4 REMEMBER WHAT JESUS DID FOR YOU

Just think of {Jesus} Who endured from sinners such grievous opposition and bitter hostility against Himself [reckon up and consider it all in comparison with your trials], so that you may not grow weary or exhausted, losing heart and relaxing and fainting in your minds.

—Hebrews 12:3 AMP
{Word in brackets added for clarity.}

Jesus lived relentlessly. He endured troubles and trials just like we do, and He overcame them by the power of God's grace. Remembering what He went through for us is good medicine for weariness of heart and soul. Hebrews 12:2-3 in The Message says,

> Keep your eyes on Jesus, who both began and finished this race we're in. **Study how he did it.** Because he never lost sight of where he was headed—that exhilarating finish in and with God—he could put up with anything along the way: Cross, shame, whatever. And now he's there, in the place of honor, right alongside God.
> When you find yourselves flagging in your faith, go over that story again, item by item, that long litany of hostility he plowed through. That will shoot adrenaline into your souls!

Take time to read one of the gospel accounts of Christ's final few hours before His death. You'll find them here: Matthew 26:57-75, 27:1-50 • Mark 14:53-72, 15:1-37 • Luke 22:54-71, 23:1-46 • John 18:12-40, 19:1-30. For an even greater understanding, read each one.

How does Jesus' suffering and sacrifice minister to you personally?

_____

_____

How does remembering Jesus' story encourage you to continue on?

_____

_____

_____

What else is the Holy Spirit speaking to you? Is He prompting you to make any changes in your attitude or perspective? If so, what are they?

_____

_____

_____

_____

For Further Study...
THE SUFFERING SERVANT:
Isaiah 53:1-12
EXALTED TO THE HIGHEST
PLACE: Philippians 2:5-11

Day 5 LET TROUBLE BRING TRANSFORMATION

*And we are being **transformed** into his likeness with ever-increasing glory, which comes from the Lord, who is the Spirit.*

—2 Corinthians 3:18 NIV

God's Word says, "Jesus, being *filled* with the Holy Spirit, was led by the Spirit into the wilderness" (Luke 4:1 NKJV). We too will be led by the Holy Spirit into the desert. We will experience a time of testing when there seems to be no growth, everything is dry, and the heat is turned up.

After the cycle of temptation was ended, Scripture says Jesus "returned *in the power of the Spirit*" (Luke 4:14 NKJV). Notice He went into the trial *filled with* the Spirit and came out of the trial *in the power of* the Spirit. Between His entrance and exit was **transformation**.

The word *transformed* in 2 Corinthians 3:18 is the Greek word *metamorpho*. It is a combination of the words *meta* and *morphoo*. *Meta* carries the idea of *an exchange*, and *morphoo* is the Greek word for a person's *outward form*. Put together, these two words mean "to transfigure or transform one's appearance."[12]

Carefully read Luke 4:1-14 (in more than one Bible version if possible).

How did Satan *attack* Jesus in the desert? How does He attack you?

_____

_____

_____

How did Jesus *respond*? What can you learn to apply in your life?

_____

_____

_____

Are you facing the same tests over and over without success? Ask God to show you what adjustments are needed in your life in order to experience the transformation He desires. Write what He speaks to you.

_____

_____

_____

[For my determined purpose is]...that I may so share His sufferings as to be **continually transformed** *[in spirit into His likeness even] to His death.*
—Philippians 3:10 AMP

Day 6 KNOW THAT GOD IS FOR YOU!

What then shall we say to [all] this? If God is for us, who [can be] against us? [Who can be our foe, if God is on our side?]

—Romans 8:31 AMP

God is for us! Wow. What a powerful statement of truth—a statement that deserves our attention. Max Lucado helps us soak in this truth:

"Read slowly the phrase, 'God is for us.' Please pause for a minute before you continue. Read it again, aloud. (My apologies to the person next to you.) *God is for us.* Repeat the phrase four times, this time emphasizing each word. (Come on, you're not in that big of a hurry.)

God is for us. God **is** for us. God is **for** us. God is for **us.**

God is for you. Your parents may have forgotten you, your teachers may have neglected you, your siblings may be ashamed of you; but within reach of your prayers is the maker of the oceans. God!

God *is* for you. Not 'may be,' not 'has been,' not 'was,' not 'would be,' but 'God is!' He *is* for you. Today. At this hour. At this minute. As you read this sentence. No need to wait in line or come back tomorrow. He is with you. He could not be closer than he is at this second. His loyalty won't increase if you are better nor lessen if you are worse. He *is* for you."[13]

God is for you! What do these four words speak to your heart right now?

Who or what is against you right now? How does focusing on the fact that *God is for you* help you have a clearer, more hopeful view of the situation?

Slowly read David's words in Psalm 18:1-19 when God delivered him from his enemies. How can you identify with him? What image of God do his words create? How are you encouraged?

For Further Study...
Psalm 3:3-8, 20:6-7, 27:1-5, 118:6-7; Isaiah 41:10-14; Hebrews 13:5-6

SESSION SUMMARY

The Kingdom of God is not a physical place but a manifestation of His power and character. God doesn't just want us to *see*, or be aware of, His Kingdom— He wants us to *enter* it. He wants us to *arise and come into* His supreme, powerful rule experientially. We do this in times of tribulation. If handled correctly, trouble will transform us into the image of Christ and elevate us to a higher level of ruling in life.

Notes

_____

(1) Adapted from *Strong's Exhaustive Concordance of the Bible*, James Strong, LL.D., S.T.D. (Nashville, TN: Thomas Nelson Publishers, 1990). (2) Adapted from *Relentless*, John Bevere (Colorado Springs, CO: WaterBrook Press, 2011) p. 64. (3) Dr. Miles Munroe, *Understanding the Purpose and Power of Prayer* (New Kensington, PA: Whitaker House, 2002) p. 120. (4) See note 1. (5) Ibid. (6) Adapted from *Thayer's Greek-English Lexicon of the New Testament*, Joseph H. Thayer (Grand Rapids, MI: Baker Book House Company, 1977) p. 291. (7) Adapted from *Relentless*, John Bevere (Colorado Springs, CO: WaterBrook Press, 2011) p. 69. (8) Hannah Whitall Smith, *The Christian's Secret of a Happy Life* (Gainesville, FL: Bridge-Logos, 1998) p. 127. (9) David Jeremiah, *Captured by Grace* (Nashville, TN: Thomas Nelson, Inc., 2006) p. 90. (10) Mother Teresa, *No Greater Love* (Novato, CA: New World Library, 1997, 2001) pp. 136-137. (11) Smith Wigglesworth, *Faith That Prevails* (Springfield, MO: Gospel Publishing House, 1938, 1966) p. 36. (12) Adapted from *Sparkling Gems from the Greek*, Rick Renner (Tulsa, OK: Teach All Nations, 2003) p. 644. (13) Max Lucado, *In the Grip of Grace* (Dallas, TX: Word Publishing, 1996) pp. 173-174.

The thief's purpose is to steal and kill and destroy. My purpose is to give them a rich and satisfying life.

—John 10:10 NLT

Chapter 5

WHO'S BEHIND THE TROUBLE?

Please refer to session 5 of the teaching series, along with chapter 7 in the Relentless book.

G 1. As believers, it's important to realize we are spiritual soldiers in a spiritual war. We all go through basic training and are equipped with special gear to empower and protect us. Carefully read these verses. What wisdom and insight is the Holy Spirit showing you to help you be a better soldier?

> We are human, but we don't wage war with human plans and methods. We use God's mighty weapons, not mere worldly weapons, to knock down the Devil's strongholds.
>
> —*2 Corinthians 10:3-4 NLT*

> Put on God's whole armor [the armor of a heavy-armed soldier which God supplies], that you may be able successfully to stand up against [all] the strategies and the deceits of the devil. ...This is no afternoon athletic contest that we'll walk away from and forget about in a couple of hours. This is for keeps, a life-or-death fight to the finish against the Devil and all his angels.
>
> —*Ephesians 6:11-12, AMP & The Message*

> Take your share of suffering as a good soldier of Jesus Christ, just as I do, and as Christ's soldier do not let yourself become tied up in worldly affairs, for then you cannot satisfy the one who has enlisted you in his army.
>
> —*2 Timothy 2:3-4 TLB*

SETTING *the* PACE

"Every disciple must know that his warfare is *not* physical, natural, or carnal. ... Your battle is in the spiritual world against the rulers of darkness. An aggressive warfare is being waged on all fronts by unseen and formidable foes. The Church must exercise dominion over the powers of the spiritual world in order to reach the masses of this generation for Christ."
—**Lester Sumrall**[1]

The wicked flee when no one pursues,
but the righteous are bold as a lion.
—Proverbs 28:1 NKJV

2. God wants us to *fight the good fight of faith,* [G] holding tightly to the eternal life to which He has called us (see 1 Timothy 6:12). He doesn't want us to take the path of a coward, avoiding or fleeing the fight. Instead, He wants us to take the path of a hero, boldly facing and winning the fight.

Ponder these promises from the Lord.

But I thank God, who always leads us in victory because of Christ.
—2 Corinthians 2:14 GW

Overwhelming victory is ours through Christ, who loved us.
—Romans 8:37 NLT

Everyone who has been born from God has won the victory over the world. Our faith is what wins the victory over the world.
—1 John 5:4 GW

SETTING
the PACE

"As part of Christ's army, you march in the ranks of gallant spirits. Every one of your fellow soldiers is the child of a King. Some, like you, are in the midst of battle, besieged on every side by affliction and temptation. Others, after many assaults, repulses, and rallyings of their faith, are already standing upon the wall of heaven as conquerors. From there they look down and urge you, their comrades on earth, to march up the hill after them. This is their cry: '**Fight** to the death and the City is your own, as now it is ours!'"
—William Gurnall[2]

But no weapon that is formed against you shall prosper, and every tongue that shall rise against you in judgment you shall show to be in the wrong. This [peace, righteousness, security, triumph over opposition] is the heritage of the servants of the Lord [those in whom the ideal Servant of the Lord is reproduced]; this is the righteousness or the vindication which they obtain from Me [this is that which I impart to them as their justification], says the Lord.
—Isaiah 54:17 AMP

What is the recurring theme in these verses? How do they stir your heart?

_____

_____

_____

_____

_____

Group leader extra: Luke 10:19

*Such a large crowd of witnesses is all around us! So we must get rid
of everything that slows us down, especially the sin that just won't let go.
And we must be determined to run the race that is ahead of us.*
—Hebrews 12:1 CEV

3. Jesus told His disciples to get into the boat and go to the other side—not go
    halfway and be destroyed by a storm. They had *His word* that they would
    make it. Having God's word on something means it's a done deal. Do you
    have God's word of direction on something but haven't stepped out into it
    yet? If so, what is it, and what is holding you back?

    _____

    _____

    _____

    _____

Group leader extras: Luke 4:1-4; Matthew 14:25-32.

*Man does not live by bread only, but man lives by every word
that proceeds out of the mouth of the Lord.*
—Deuteronomy 8:3 AMP

4. When you *face and fight* the storms of life, great
    victory is won. Look back over the trials in your
    life. What wisdom that is helping you today did
    you acquire by going through tough situations?
    Whose lives have been positively impacted
    because you suffered and passed the test?
    How have they been helped?

> **CORE STRENGTHENER**
>
> God will never lead you into
> a storm that He doesn't give
> you the power—the grace—
> to overcome. Brand this
> truth forever on your heart,
> for it will strengthen you
> when you face adversity.

The *wisdom* God has taught me through tough
times:

_____

_____

_____

_____

The *people* who've been helped because I relentlessly persevered:

_____

_____

_____

_____

_____

What a wonderful God we have—he is the Father of our Lord Jesus Christ,
the source of every mercy, and the one who so wonderfully comforts and
strengthens us in our hardships and trials. And why does he do this?
So that when others are troubled, needing our sympathy and encouragement,
we can pass on to them this same help and comfort God has given us.
—2 Corinthians 1:3-4 TLB

SETTING *the* PACE

"No matter what hardship, devilish plot, or accusation is hurled our way, every- thing Satan would use to destroy is redeemed by God's love; then it is used to perfect us. If we faithfully seek the Lord, adversity becomes like gasoline on our heart's fire for God."
—Francis Frangipane[3]

5. God is **not** the source, designer, or instigator of the hardships (*thlipsis*) you face—Satan and his demonic forces are. Why is it imperative for you to know this? What will happen if you think God is behind it?

_____

_____

_____

_____

_____

_____

_____

_____

G 6. Identifying the source of trials and temptations has been a stumbling block for many. Take time to meditate on James 1:13-17. How does this passage help you *know that you know* God is not the source of your trouble? From where does the desire to sin originate?

> Don't let anyone under pressure to give in to evil say, "God is trying to trip me up." God is impervious to evil, and puts evil in no one's way.
>
> The temptation [desire] to give in to evil comes from us and only us. We have no one to blame but the leering, seducing flare-up of our own lust. Lust gets pregnant, and has a baby: sin! Sin grows up to adulthood, and becomes a real killer.
>
> So, my very dear friends, don't get thrown off course. Every desirable and beneficial gift comes out of heaven. The gifts are rivers of light cascading down from the Father of Light. There is nothing deceitful in God, nothing two-faced, nothing fickle.
>
> **—James 1:13-17 The Message**
> [Word in brackets added for clarity.]

_____

_____

_____

_____

The thief comes only in order to steal and kill and destroy. I came that they may have and enjoy life, and have it in abundance (to the full, till it overflows).
—John 10:10 AMP

7. *Guilt* and *shame* are major tools the enemy uses against us to keep us from advancing God's Kingdom. Thankfully, Jesus has not only set us free from sin but also from the shame and guilt that come with it. What insights can you draw from these life-giving truths and how can you use them against the enemy?

CORE STRENGTHENER

It's crystal clear: Any hardship that falls under the category of killing, stealing, or destroying, the enemy is behind—he is the source. On the other hand, God's purpose for you is *life* in all its fullness. When faced with pressure, hardship, or suffering of any kind, **use the filter of John 10:10** to determine if it is God or the enemy who's behind it.

As the Scripture says, "Anyone who trusts in him will never be put to shame."
—*Romans 10:11 NIV*

And such some of you were [once]. But you were washed clean (purified by a complete atonement for sin and made free from the guilt of sin), and you were consecrated (set apart, hallowed), and you were justified [pronounced righteous, by trusting] in the name of the Lord Jesus Christ and in the [Holy] Spirit of our God.
—*1 Corinthians 6:11 AMP*

But if we [really] are living and walking in the Light, as He [Himself] is in the Light, we have [true, unbroken] fellowship with one another, and the blood of Jesus Christ His Son cleanses (removes) us from all sin and guilt [keeps us cleansed from sin in all its forms and manifestations].
—*1 John 1:7 AMP*

GUILT – SHAME – CONDEMNATION

Guilt in the truest sense is "a crime, offense, or debt." It is from a root word meaning "to pay." The guilt of a person exists once he knowingly violates a law and makes him a debtor to the law. **Shame** is "a painful sensation excited by a consciousness of guilt; an action bringing disgrace or dishonor, causing the face to blush." **Condemnation** is the act of condemning, which means "to pronounce utterly wrong or guilty; to doom or sentence to punishment; it implies utter rejection."[4]

Who dares accuse us whom God has chosen for his own? Will God? No!
He is the one who has forgiven us and given us right standing with himself.
Who then will condemn us? Will Christ? No! For he is the one who died
for us and came back to life again for us and is sitting at the place of
highest honor next to God, pleading for us there in heaven.
—Romans 8:33-34 TLB

8. In addition to being free from guilt and shame, we're also free from con-
    demnation. Name the three main areas where the enemy tries to make you
    feel condemned.

    _____

    _____

    _____

The next time the enemy tries to accuse you for sins you have already
repented of, speak the Word back to him. **Meditate on the message** of
these truths and *speak them* against the enemy!

There is therefore now no condemnation to me...in Christ Jesus, because I do
not walk according to my flesh, but according to the leading of the Holy Spirit.
For the law of the Spirit of life in Christ Jesus has made me free from the law
of sin and death.

—Romans 8:1-2 NKJV

For God did not send the Son into my life in order to judge (to reject, to condemn, to pass sentence on) me, but that I might find salvation and be made
safe and sound through Him. Because I believe in Him [I cling to, trust in, and
rely on Him], I am not judged [I who trust in Him never come up for judgment;
for me there is no rejection, no condemnation—I incur
no damnation].

—John 3:17-18 AMP
{Personalized for emphasis.}

Group leader extras: Isaiah 50:9; John 5:24.

CORE STRENGTHENER

Settle this now: *You are for-*
given in Christ Jesus. There
is no sin you've committed
that is not eradicated by
His blood! So if shame,
guilt, or condemnation
arises in your soul over
something you've thought,
said, or done in the past,
and you've already asked
for God's forgiveness, then
God is not behind it.

9. Sickness is *not* from God—health is. Read the
    stories of blind Bartimaeus and the Canaanite
    woman in Matthew 15:21-28 and Mark 10:46-52.
    What can you learn from their relentless pursuit
    and apply to your own life?

    _____

    _____

    _____

    _____

10. More than anything, God wants you, His child, to prosper and be in health (see 3 John 1:2). He is *not* the source of illness or financial struggles, but He does use them to position us in greater authority.

The Bible repeatedly calls us overcomers. To overcome is "to get the better of in a conflict; to render incapable or powerless; to surmount (obstacles, objections, etc.); to be victorious."[5] How would you communicate an overcomer's perspective to someone struggling with condemnation, health, or finances?

Condemnation

_____

_____

_____

_____

Health

_____

_____

_____

_____

Finances

_____

_____

_____

_____

_____

_____

_____

CORE STRENGTHENER

Remember, any opposition that falls under the categories of theft, death, or destruction has nothing to do with God. It is from the forces of Satan who want to discourage, defeat, and devour you. We must battle them relentlessly in order to see God's Kingdom manifest on earth as it is in heaven.

Weekly CHALLENGE

Identify an area of trouble in which you are uncertain of God's will. Study the Scriptures for promises or revelations that reveal His heart in the matter. Write or type out these verses and post them in visible locations. Speak them aloud whenever you are confronted by difficulty or doubt.

Day 1 **KNOW GOD LOVES YOU**

But God is so rich in mercy, and he loved us so much, that even though we were dead because of our sins, he gave us life when he raised Christ from the dead. (It is only by God's grace that you have been saved!)

—Ephesians 2:4-5 NLT

Most of us know that John 3:16 says, "For God so loved the world" (NKJV). But do you know that His love is *everlasting*? In Jeremiah 31:3 God says, "I have loved you with an everlasting love; I have drawn you with loving-kindness" (NIV). God's love is eternal—so powerful and great that it has no beginning or end!

How can you know God loves you? *Take Him at His Word*. Don't follow your feelings or listen to the enemy. **Meditate on the message** of these passages:

God's **love** has been poured out in our hearts through the Holy Spirit Who has been given to us. While we were yet in weakness [powerless to help ourselves], at the fitting time Christ died for (in behalf of) the ungodly. Now it is an extraordinary thing for one to give his life even for an upright man, though perhaps for a noble and lovable and generous benefactor someone might even dare to die. But God shows and clearly proves His [own] love for us by the fact that **while we were still sinners**, Christ (the Messiah, the Anointed One) died for us.

—*Romans 5:5-8 AMP*

Once we, too, were foolish and disobedient. We were misled and became slaves to many lusts and pleasures. Our lives were full of evil and envy, and we hated each other. But—"When God our Savior **revealed his kindness and love**, he saved us, not because of the righteous things we had done, but because of his mercy. He washed away our sins, giving us a new birth and new life through the Holy Spirit. He generously poured out the Spirit upon us through Jesus Christ our Savior. Because of his grace he declared us righteous and gave us confidence that we will inherit eternal life."

—*Titus 3:3-7 NLT*

Read Romans 8. When you disobey or lack faith, how does God see you?

_____

Pause and ponder God's great love for you. Then write out a paragraph of praise for all He's done.

_____
_____
_____
_____
_____

Day 2 **KNOW YOUR ENEMY**

Satan will not outsmart us...for we are familiar with his evil schemes.
—2 Corinthians 2:11 NLT

A soldier going to war is trained to know who he is fighting. The more he is aware of his enemy's strategies, the more skilled the soldier is. The same is true for us as believers. How can we be familiar with Satan's evil schemes? Through the filter Jesus gave us in John 10:10: "The thief's purpose is to steal and kill and destroy. My purpose is to give...a rich and satisfying life" (NLT). Rick Renner dissects the meaning of a few key words in this passage.

> The word thief is the Greek word klepto, which means "to steal." It gives us the image of a bandit or pickpocket who is so artful in the way he steals that his exploits of thievery are nearly undetectable. Jesus uses this word to let us know the devil is so sly and deceptive that he often accomplishes his goal before a person realizes what's happened.
>
> The words to kill are from the Greek word thuo, which originally referred to "the sacrificial giving of animals on the altar—something that is precious and dear." It had nothing to do with murder. By Jesus' use of this word, He is saying that if the thief hasn't already walked away with everything we hold dear, he will try to convince us to sacrifice everything he has not already taken.
>
> The third phrase Jesus uses to describe the enemy's goal is to destroy. Destroy is from the Greek word apollumi and carries with it the idea of "something that is ruined, wasted, trashed and devastated." Here, Jesus is telling us that if Satan cannot steal from us or convince us to sacrifice that which we hold dear in order to have peace, he will try to totally ruin and devastate it.
>
> Make no mistake, if the enemy is not stopped, he will rob us blind, make us sacrifice everything good God has given us in order to have peace, and totally obliterate our lives.[6]

What is the Holy Spirit revealing to you about the enemy and his attacks on your life?

_____

_____

_____

Read John 8:44. What mode of Satan's operation does He point out and how can you arm yourself against it?

_____

_____

_____

Day 3 COOPERATE WITH GOD'S CORRECTION

My dear child, don't shrug off God's discipline, but don't be crushed by it either.
It's the child he loves that he disciplines; the child he embraces, he also corrects.

—Hebrews 12:5-6 The Message

Discipline is the divine link between desire and destiny—it's the bridge that gets us where we want to go. James Dobson adequately stated, "If one examines the secret behind a championship football team, a magnificent orchestra, or a successful business, the principal ingredient is invariably discipline."[7]

Interestingly, God's discipline and condemnation from the enemy are both uncomfortable and at times downright painful. However, there is a big difference between the two. Condemnation does *not* give us a way out. It only leaves us with guilt and shame. In contrast, God's correction does give us a way out, and it's called *repentance*. He corrects us out of love to restore our fellowship and mature us into the likeness of Jesus.

According to Hebrews 12:10-11, what are the **blessings** of cooperating with God's correction?

_____

_____

What do Jesus and Malachi compare God's correction to? How should we cooperate with Him?
Read John 15:1-8 • Malachi 3:1-4

_____

See also: Zechariah 13:8-9

Our goal is to *not* sin by God's empowering grace. But *if* we do sin, we're to deal with it quickly. *Read* 1 John 1:9, Psalm 32:1-6, and Proverbs 28:13. In your own words, describe the response of true repentance.

_____

_____

_____

What can you know with certainty God will do when you repent? How does this encourage you?
Read Psalm 103:2-3, 12 • 1 John 1:9; 2:1-2 • 1 Peter 2:24 • Colossians 2:13-15

_____

For Further Study...
Deuteronomy 8:5; Job 5:17;
Psalm 94:12-13, 119:67;
Proverbs 3:11-12; Acts 3:19

Day 4 CULTIVATE A HEALTHY CONSCIOUSNESS

The blood of Christ, who had no defect, does even more. Through the eternal Spirit he offered himself to God and **cleansed our consciences** *from the useless things we had done. Now we can serve the living God.*

—Hebrews 9:14 GW

When it comes to sin and our conscience, two options are before us: we can be either *sin conscious* or *righteousness conscious*. **Sin consciousness** is seeing ourselves as "just a sinner saved by grace," constantly aware of every fault and failure. It is a breeding ground for guilt, shame, and condemnation.

On the other hand, a **consciousness of righteousness** keeps Christ's victory over sin at the forefront of our minds. It means that we know we are at right standing with God. We are aware that sin's power was completely broken off our lives through Christ's finished work on the cross, and that His grace gives us the power to walk free of sin inside and out. When we are conscious of our righteousness, we are perfectly positioned to grow in the power of grace.

Try this test. Do not think about snakes. Forget every picture you've seen of cobras coiled back and ready to strike. Put out of your mind images of huge boa constrictors and pits filled with rattlesnakes. Just don't think about their scaly, slithering bodies. Did it work? No. In fact, you thought of them more, right? That's because you became "snake conscious."

So what happens when you focus on past sins and weaknesses? Who do you think is reminding you of these failures (see Revelation 12:10; Zechariah 3:1-2)? What should you do about it?

_____

_____

Focus on and declare aloud who you are in Christ! Read each verse and write a brief, personalized statement that proclaims that you are in right standing with God.

Philippians 3:9 *I am in Christ, and my righteousness comes from God by faith.*

2 Corinthians 5:21 _____

Romans 6:6-7, 14 _____

Romans 8:1-2 _____

_____

Ephesians 2:1, 4-6 _____

_____

Related Scriptures: 1 Corinthians 1:30; 2 Corinthians 5:17; Galatians 3:13; Ephesians 1:7; Colossians 1:13-14.

For Further Study...
Acts 24:16; 1 Corinthians 8:7-13; 1 Timothy 1:5, 18-19; 4:1-2; Titus 1:15-16; Hebrews 9:14; 10:19-22; 1 Peter 3:15-16

Day 5 GOD HEALS

*"If you are willing, you can heal me and make me clean," he said. ...Jesus reached out and touched him. "**I am willing**," he said. "Be healed!"*
—Mark 1:40-41 NLT

Throughout the New Testament, countless people came to Jesus and His disciples for healing. No one was turned away. Scripture says the people brought to Jesus "all who were sick. And whatever their sickness or disease...he healed them all" (Matthew 4:24 NLT).

Since Jesus is the exact image of the Father (Colossians 1:15; Hebrews 1:3), only does the Father's will (John 5:19-20), and is the same yesterday, today, and forever (Hebrews 13:8), what does this say about God's desire for your healing?

_____

Healing is just as much a part of redemption as forgiveness. **Slowly read aloud** these amazing, personalized promises.

He forgives all *my* **sins** and heals all my **diseases**.
—*Psalm 103:2-3 NLT*

Surely He has borne *my* griefs (**sicknesses**, **weaknesses**, and **distresses**) and... with the stripes [that wounded] Him *I* am **healed** and **made whole**.
—*Isaiah 53:4-5 AMP*

He personally bore *my* sins in His [own] body on the tree [as on an altar and offered Himself on it]... By His wounds *I* have been healed.
—*1 Peter 2:24 AMP*

What is the Holy Spirit speaking to you in these verses?

_____

_____

Are you struggling to believe for someone's healing? What is the greatest obstacle to your faith? Why should your faith be based on His Word, not experience?

_____

_____

For Further Study...

HEALING (GENERAL)	JESUS HEALED ALL WHO CAME	THE APOSTLES HEALED
Exodus 15:26, 23:25-26	Matthew 4:23-24; 8:16-17; 12:15	Acts 3:1-10; 5:12-16; 9:32-42
Psalm 107:19-20	Matthew 14:35-36	Acts 14:8-10; 19:11-12
Proverbs 4:20-22, 3 John 1:2	Mark 3:7-12; Luke 4:40; 6:19	Acts 28:7-9

Day 6 **BELIEVE GOD WILL PROVIDE**

And God will generously provide all you need. Then you will always have everything you need and plenty left over to share with others.

—**2 Corinthians 9:8 NLT**

God's grace is also *financial provision*. As we faithfully give Him our time, talent, and treasure, He will faithfully give us what we need. He will provide for us according to *His* limitless riches, not how well the stock market is doing, the condition of our economy, or how much money we have in savings.

Meditate on the message of these powerful promises.

And my God will liberally supply (fill to the full) your every need according to His riches in glory in Christ Jesus.

—*Philippians 4:19 AMP*

There is no want to those who truly revere and worship Him with godly fear. The young lions lack food and suffer hunger, but they who seek (inquire of and require) the Lord [by right of their need and on the authority of His Word], none of them shall lack any beneficial thing.

—*Psalm 34:9-10 AMP*

I have been young and now I am old. And in all my years I have never seen the Lord forsake a man who loves him; nor have I seen the children of the godly go hungry.

—*Psalm 37:25 TLB*

No good thing will the Lord withhold from those who do what is right.

—*Psalm 84:11 NLT*

And God is able to make all grace (every favor and earthly blessing) come to you in abundance, so that you may always and under all circumstances and whatever the need be self-sufficient [possessing enough to require no aid or support and furnished in abundance for every good work and charitable donation].

—*2 Corinthians 9:8 AMP*

What is the Lord speaking to you in these verses? How do they ignite your faith?

Carefully read Luke 6:38, Ecclesiastes 11:1, Proverbs 11:25, and Malachi 3:10-12. What important principles about receiving God's provision can you draw from these scriptures?

_____

_____

_____

Consider 2 Corinthians 9:8-12 and, in your own words, describe true prosperity and how it brings God glory.

_____

_____

_____

_____

> **For Further Study...**
> Deuteronomy 8:18, 28:12;
> Psalm 103:5; Ephesians
> 3:20; Hebrews 13:5;
> 1 Timothy 6:10

SESSION SUMMARY

We are spiritual soldiers in a spiritual war. As we fight the good fight of faith, we will encounter a number of hardships. God is *not* the source, designer, or instigator of hardships you face—Satan and his demonic forces are. By God's grace, we are to relentlessly stand against all opposition that comes to steal, kill, or destroy what God has entrusted to us.

(1) Dr. Lester Sumrall, *Faith Can Change Your World* (South Bend, IN: Sumrall Publishing, 1999) p. 187. (2) John Eldredge, *Wild at Heart* (Nashville, TN: Thomas Nelson Publishers, 2001) p. 156. (3) Francis Frangipane, *The Shelter of the Most High* (Lake Mary, FL: Charisma House, A Strang Company, 2008) p. 156. (4) Adapted from *Noah Webster's First Edition of an American Dictionary of the English Language* (1828), Republished in facsimile edition by Foundation for American Christian Education (San Francisco, CA 2000). (5) overcome. Dictionary.com. *Collins English Dictionary - Complete & Unabridged 10th Edition*. HarperCollins Publishers. http://dictionary.reference.com/browse/overcome(accessed: July 14, 2011). (6) Adapted from *Sparkling Gems from the Greek*, Rick Renner (Tulsa, OK: Teach All Nations, 2003) pp. 547-548. (7) *Fast Break, Five-Minute Devotions to Start Your Day* (St. San Luis Obispo, CA: Parable, 2007) Day 272. (8)Adapted from *Vine's Complete Expository Dictionary of Old and New Testament Words*, W.E. Vine (Nashville, TN: Thomas Nelson Publishing, 1996). (9) *The Quotable Lewis*, Wayne Martindale and Jerry Root, Editors (Carol Stream, IL: Tyndale House Publishers, Inc. 1990) p 407.

Notes

Therefore, since Christ suffered for us in the flesh, **arm yourselves** *also with the same mind, for he who has suffered in the flesh has ceased from sin.*

—1 Peter 4:1 NKJV

6

ARM YOURSELF

Please refer to session 6 of the teaching series,
along with chapter 8 in the Relentless book.

G 1. The specific suffering Jesus endured was *unfair treatment* from people. Thankfully, He left us a personal example we can follow when we face the same. Carefully read these verses. What can you learn about responding to hardship to apply in your life by God's grace?

CORE STRENGTHENER

Many believers are unarmed. When unexpected tribulations (*thlipsis*) strike, they're caught off guard and enter a state of shock, bewilderment, or amazement. As a result, they *react* instead of *act*. Peter, under the inspiration of the Holy Spirit, admonishes us to **arm ourselves** to suffer in the same manner as Christ did.

> Then Jesus said to His disciples, If anyone desires to be My disciple, let him deny himself [disregard, lose sight of, and forget himself and his own interests] and take up his cross and follow Me [cleave steadfastly to Me, conform wholly to My example in living and, if need be, in dying, also]. For whoever is bent on saving his [temporal] life [his comfort and security here] shall lose it [eternal life]; and whoever loses his life [his comfort and security here] for My sake shall find it [life everlasting].
> —*Matthew 16:24-25 AMP*

He never sinned, nor ever deceived anyone. He did not retaliate when he was insulted, nor threaten revenge when he suffered. He left his case in the hands of God, who always judges fairly.

—*1 Peter 2:22-23 NLT*

He was abused and punished, but he didn't open his mouth. He was led like a lamb to the slaughter. He was like a sheep that is silent when its wool is cut off. He didn't open his mouth.

—*Isaiah 53:7 GW*

Don't repay evil for evil. Don't retaliate with insults when people insult you. Instead, pay them back with a blessing. That is what God has called you to do, and he will bless you for it. For the Scriptures say, "If you want to enjoy life and see many happy days, keep your tongue from speaking evil and your lips from telling lies. Turn away from evil and do good. Search for peace, and work to maintain it.

—1 Peter 3:9-11 NLT

Group leader extras: Matthew 11:28-30, Hebrews 12:2.

This is the kind of life you've been invited into, the kind of life Christ lived. He suffered everything that came his way so you would know that it could be done, and also know how to do it, step-by-step.
—1 Peter 2:21 The Message

G 2. God's Word plainly states that if we live godly lives, we're going to suffer hardship and persecution. However, if a person is a Christian in name only and *lives like the rest of the world*, he will *not* be persecuted. Why is this— why does Satan leave them alone? If you *are* going through hardship, what can you know with confidence?

SETTING *the* PACE

"God, who foresaw your tribulation, has specifically *armed you* to go through it, not without pain but without stain."
—*C.S. Lewis*[1]

Four Principles with which to Arm Yourself
1. Tribulation is inevitable.
2. The troubles you face are nothing new.
3. You never have to lose a battle.
4. God's grace in your life is sufficient to win every battle you are going to face.

3. Just as commercial pilots are rigorously and regularly trained in a flight simulator, God is training and arming us through the tests He allows in our lives. As out of control as things may seem, *God is always in control of the test.* Carefully meditate on the message of 1 Corinthians 10:13. What insight can you gather from this extraordinary promise?

The temptations in your life are no different from what others experience. And God is faithful. He will not allow the temptation to be more than you can stand. When you are tempted, he will show you a way out so that you can endure.

NLT

No test or temptation that comes your way is beyond the course of what others have had to face. All you need to remember is that God will never let you down; he'll never let you be pushed past your limit; he'll always be there to help you come through it.

The Message

There isn't any temptation that you have experienced which is unusual for humans. God, who faithfully keeps his promises, will not allow you to be tempted beyond your power to resist. But when you are tempted, he will also give you the ability to endure the temptation as your way of escape.

GW

_____

_____

_____

The Lord knows how to rescue godly people from their sufferings and to punish evil people while they wait for the day of judgment.
—2 Peter 2:9 CEV

CORE STRENGTHENER

The devil does not have free access to you. His attacks must first be passed through the permission of the Almighty. Your heavenly Father will never author or instigate the tests, but He will sometimes allow them so you can beat up the enemy and bring glory to Him as you take ground for the Kingdom.

G 4. Has the enemy ever whispered something like this to you? *Nobody knows what you're going through. Nobody is dealing with what you're dealing with. You've got it so bad.* If so, consider 1 Corinthians 10:13 again along with these truths from Scripture.

Stand firm against him {Satan}, and be strong in your faith. Remember that your Christian brothers and sisters all over the world are going through the same kind of suffering you are.

—1 Peter 5:9 NLT

History merely repeats itself. It has all been done before. Nothing under the sun is truly new.

—Ecclesiastes 1:9 NLT

So we have been greatly encouraged in the midst of our troubles and suffering, dear brothers and sisters, because you have remained strong in your faith. It gives us new life to know that you are standing firm in the Lord.

—1 Thessalonians 3:7-8 NLT
{Word in brackets added for clarity.}

How does knowing other believers in the world are facing the same trials strengthen you to endure?

Group leader extra: Remember Jesus' sobering statement in John 8:44.

 5. Imagine you just led a coworker to the Lord—someone you've been praying for, for a long time. Why is it important to let them know that as a follower of Christ they will face troubles? What else can you say to encourage them and give them a balanced perspective of the true hope they have in Christ?

Group leader extra: Consider the parable of the sower in Mark 4:14-20 and Matthew 13:18-23.

SETTING *the* PACE

"Trials that often come into a Christian's life are the fulfillment of God's gracious purpose as He seeks to make us the sort of person He planned for us to be when He first thought of us. Like a sculptor, He begins with a lump of marble. But He has in mind a picture of what He intends to create. He breaks, cracks, chisels, and polishes until one day there emerges His vision. ...At the moment, His sculpture of us is incomplete. God has not finished with us."
—*Billy Graham*[2]

6. Another principle to arm us in our fight against the enemy is that *we never have to lose*. We've been given superior power and authority in Christ and are seated with Him far above all the power of Satan and his fallen angels.

Meditate on the message of these promises from your heavenly Father.

Behold! I have given you authority and power to trample upon serpents and scorpions, and [physical and mental strength and ability] over all the power that the enemy [possesses]; and nothing shall in any way harm you.
—*Luke 10:19 AMP*

Little children, you are of God [you belong to Him] and have [already] defeated and overcome them [the agents of the antichrist], because He Who lives in you is greater (mightier) than he who is in the world.
—*1 John 4:4 AMP*

I want you to know about the great and mighty power that God has for us followers. It is the same wonderful power he used when he raised Christ from death and let him sit at his right side in heaven. There Christ rules over all forces, authorities, powers, and rulers. He rules over all beings in this world and will rule in the future world as well. God has put all things under the power of Christ, and for the good of the church he has made him the head of everything.
—*Ephesians 1:19-22 CEV*

"No weapon that has been made to be used against you will succeed. You will have an answer for anyone who accuses you. This is the inheritance of the Lord's servants. Their victory comes from me," declares the Lord.

—*Isaiah 54:17 GW*

How do these truths arm and encourage you to fight against the enemy?

_____

_____

_____

_____

Group leader extras: 2 Corinthians 2:14; 1 John 5:4.

7. All resistance from the enemy is an opportunity for two positive things to take place. Carefully consider these words from Peter and James and identify these two blessings.

> Dear friends, don't be surprised at the fiery trials you are going through, as if something strange were happening to you. Instead, be very glad— for these trials make you partners with Christ in his suffering, so that you will have the wonderful joy of seeing his glory when it is revealed to all the world. So be happy when you are insulted for being a Christian, for then the glorious Spirit of God rests upon you. But it is no shame to suffer for being a Christian. Praise God for the privilege of being called by his name! So if you are suffering in a manner that pleases God, keep on doing what is right, and trust your lives to the God who created you, for he will never fail you.

—*1 Peter 4:12-14, 16, 19 NLT*

CORE STRENGTHENER

Jesus gave us the privilege of completing His task of bringing His finished work to the ends of the earth. The enemy resists with a furious vengeance, which produces suffering, but it's a *victorious* suffering. The important point to remember is any adversity you face is something someone has already tackled and overcome.

> Consider it a sheer gift, friends, when tests and challenges come at you from all sides. You know that under pressure, your faith-life is forced into the open and shows its true colors. So don't try to get out of anything prematurely. Let it do its work so you become mature and well-developed, not deficient in any way.

—*James 1:2-4 The Message*

_____

_____

_____

_____

Group leader extra: 1 Peter 1:6-7

SETTING the PACE

"What has been the result of his constant tribulations? ... Paul has come to realize that no matter how hard you squeeze him, all you can do is help the process along—the process of transforming him to the image of Christ. There is nothing the world can throw at us that God will not use for His glory and our eternal joy."

—David Jeremiah[3]

8. Paul was given revelation about the Kingdom of God far beyond what others had experienced. But with that knowledge came a "thorn in the flesh," a messenger of Satan to torment him. Slowly read 2 Corinthians 11:23-12:10. In the context of this passage...

What does Paul himself identify his thorn in the flesh to be? (*Give attention to 11:23-33.*)

_____

_____

_____

_____

Group leader extra: Other scriptures mentioning thorns are Numbers 33:55; Joshua 23:13; Judges 2:1-3.

Where did the thorn come from? Who was it *not* from? (*Review James 1:13, 16-17.*)

_____

_____

WEAKNESSES and INFIRMITIES

Both of these words are found in 2 Corinthians 12:9, and they are from the same Greek word *asthenia*.[4] In the gospels, this word predominantly means physical sickness or disease. However, in most of Paul's letters, including 2 Corinthians, this word mainly refers to "weaknesses of human nature," specifically the human inability "to bear trials and troubles."[5] Other verses where *asthenia* is used include Romans 6:19, 8:26, and 15:1 and Hebrews 4:15.

9. Jesus' answer to Paul's prayer is the fourth principle we are to arm ourselves with: *God's grace is more than enough to win every battle.* Are you experiencing the kind of attack Paul did? Have you asked God to remove it but He hasn't? Briefly describe what you're dealing with, and then pray and ask the Lord for grace to endure and see the situation from His perspective.

_____

_____

_____

10. When the Lord answered Paul, a *paradigm shift* took place in his soul. The power of God's grace radically changed his view of the trials and tribulations

in his life. Instead of pleading with God to remove them, he welcomed them with delight in order to bring God more glory.

Meditate on these promises from God.

For I the Lord your God hold your right hand; I am the Lord, Who says to you, Fear not; I will help you! Behold, I will make you to be a new, sharp, threshing instrument which has teeth; you shall thresh the mountains and beat them small, and shall make the hills like chaff. You shall winnow them, and the wind shall carry them away, and the tempest or whirlwind shall scatter them. And you shall rejoice in the Lord, you shall glory in the Holy One of Israel.

—Isaiah 41:13, 15-16 AMP

The Lord God is my Strength, my personal bravery, and my invincible army; He makes my feet like hinds' feet and will make me to walk [not to stand still in terror, but to walk] and make [spiritual] progress upon my high places [of trouble, suffering, or responsibility]!

—Habakkuk 3:19 AMP

Who is the Rock save our God, the God who girds me with strength and makes my way perfect? He makes my feet like hinds' feet [able to stand firmly or make progress on the dangerous heights of *testing* and *trouble*]; He sets me securely upon my high places. *He teaches my hands to war*, so that my arms can bend a bow of bronze.

—Psalm 18:31-34 AMP

What is the Lord speaking to you about His desire to strengthen and change you?

_____
_____
_____
_____
_____
_____
_____
_____
_____
_____

SETTING the PACE

"Somewhere on life's path our flesh is pierced by a person or a problem. Our stride becomes a limp, our pace is slowed to a halt, we try to walk again only to wince at each effort. Finally we plead with God for help. Such was the case with Paul. ...For all we don't know about thorns, we can be sure of this. *God would prefer we have an occasional limp than a perpetual strut.* And if it takes a thorn for him to make his point, he loves us enough not to pluck it out."

—Max Lucado[6]

SETTING the PACE

"The difficulties of life do not have to be unbearable. It is the way we look at them— through faith or unbelief— that makes them seem so. We must be convinced that our Father is full of love for us and that He only permits trials to come our way for our own good."

—Brother Lawrence[7]

Do you hate hardship? Do you cringe at the thought of having to fight the enemy in difficult circumstances? Then you need a paradigm shift. Like Paul, you need God's grace to enable you to see hardships as opportunities instead of obstacles. God can bring it about supernaturally by the power of His Holy Spirit. Pray and ask Him for it.

Prayer for a New Perspective

Father, thank You for the truths You are teaching me in this session. I want to be armed against the enemy's attacks, and I want to be victorious for Your glory. Help me, Lord, to see the trials and troubles You allow in my life as opportunities to bring You glory instead of seeing them as obstacles. I need Your grace. I need You to give me a paradigm shift just like You did Paul. Strengthen me and change me from the inside out. Thank You for loving me and being patient with me as I grow. In Jesus' name, Amen.

CORE STRENGTHENER

Don't see trials as obstacles—see them as *opportunities*. We are armed when we're firmly optimistic in heart and mind regarding hardship before, during, and after the fight. We know that the war has already been won, and we have all the authority and power of heaven backing us up.

Weekly CHALLENGE

This week, pray for someone else in person and seek out personal prayer for yourself. Encourage those around you with the knowledge that they are not alone and they can overcome. Have the humility to position yourself to receive the same encouragement from the men and women of God in your life. Together, you can build a community of people who are optimistic and confident in their God-given authority.

Day 1 **FASTEN YOUR BELT OF TRUTH**

So then, take your stand! Fasten truth around your waist like a belt.
—Ephesians 6:14 GW

The first and most important piece of armor we have is the belt of truth—the doctrine of truth found in Scripture.[8] It is the written Word of God, the foundation upon which our salvation and every aspect of our new life in Christ is built.

The Roman loin belt was unattractive and virtually unnoticeable. However, it was the most vital piece of a soldier's armor, holding all the other pieces in place. The sword hung from the belt. The shield rested on the belt, and the breastplate was connected to the belt to keep it from flapping up. It also covered and protected a man's reproductive abilities.[9]

Your Bible is like the Roman loin belt. It may seem commonplace, but it is vital. Your ability to produce for God is directly tied to your relationship with His Word. It keeps you from becoming spiritually sterile. To fasten on truth like a belt is to be actively in the Word every day. Reading, studying, meditating on, and memorizing Scripture are all expressions of putting on Truth. With the Word at your core, you're armed and ready to use all your armor effectively!

Your belt is inseparably linked to your

breastplate of righteousness..Read Psalm 119:40

shoes of peace...Read Colossians 3:15-16

helmet of salvation...Read 2 Timothy 3:15-16

shield of faith...Read Romans 10:17

sword of the Spirit..Read Hebrews 4:12

With this fresh perspective on truth, how do you perceive the value of God's Word?

_____

_____

Have you ever gone days, weeks, or months *without* spending time in the Word? How did it affect your attitude, emotions, and thinking?

_____

_____

If you've noticed a decrease in your joy, peace, patience, kindness, and self-control, take a close look at how much time you've been investing in Scripture. What adjustments is the Holy Spirit prompting you to make to tighten the belt of truth?

_____

_____

_____

Day 2 PUT ON THE BREASTPLATE OF RIGHTEOUSNESS

*Stand firm then, with the belt of truth buckled around your waist, with the breast-plate of **righteousness** in place.*

—Ephesians 6:14 NIV

The *breastplate of righteousness* is the next piece of armor we are told to wear. This is the righteousness we have been given in Christ. "For our sake [*God*] made Christ [virtually] to be sin Who knew no sin, so that in and through Him we might become [endued with, viewed as being in, and examples of] the righteousness of God [what we ought to be, **approved** and **acceptable** and **in right relationship with Him**, by His goodness]" (2 Corinthians 5:21 AMP).

Righteousness defends and protects our vital organs—especially our hearts. Our hearts represent our our emotions or feelings. If we don't feel approved, acceptable, or in right standing with God, we will not successfully fight the enemy.

A Roman soldier's breastplate was the shiniest piece of armor he wore. Usually made of brass, it began at the top of the neck and extended down to the knees, covering both his front and back. The breastplate was often made of linear pieces of metal that resembled the scales of a fish. It was heavy, averaging about 40 pounds. Interestingly, the more a soldier wore his breastplate, the shinier it would become. Metal rubbed against metal creating an amazing luster in the light of the sun—blinding the enemy. Just imagine what a legion of soldiers would look like.[10]

What new insights is the Lord showing you about your breastplate of righteousness?

_____

_____

How will cultivating an attitude of righteousness affect your ability to fight?

_____

_____

What will happen if you don't *know that you know* you are the righteousness of God in Christ? How will Satan attack? How will your prayers be affected?

_____

_____

_____

By faith, put on your breastplate of righteousness! In Christ, you have been made righteous. Learn to see yourself through Jesus' finished work of the cross.

For Further Study...
Isaiah 59:17, 61:10;
1 Corinthians 1:30;
Romans 5:16-21, 10:4;
Philippians 3:9

Day 3 STRAP ON YOUR SHOES OF PEACE

Your desire to tell the good news about **peace** *should be like shoes on your feet.*
—Ephesians 6:15 CEV

Next, we are to strap on our *shoes of peace*. No matter how big or strong a soldier was or how excellently he could wield a sword, without shoes, he was left barefoot; and being barefoot in battle is a recipe for disaster.

The Roman soldier's shoes were of two parts: the shoe itself and the *greave*, a metal covering that protected the leg from the knee to the top of the foot. Inside the shoe was durable leather; outside was brass. On the underside were sharp spikes one to three inches long designed to give the soldier firm footing. These were "shod" (tied extremely tight) to the bottom of a soldier's feet.[11]

How does this imagery help you better understand your need for God's peace?

_____

_____

What do you learn from the function of the *greaves*? From the sharp spikes?

_____

_____

How has the enemy tried to *steal, kill,* or *destroy* your peace?

_____

_____

If your peace has diminished or been lost, *pause and pray.* **Meditate on the message** of these scriptures. Ask God to restore His peace, and with verbal acknowledgment, put your shoes of peace back on!

Peace I leave with you; My [own] peace I now give and bequeath to you. Not as the world gives do I give to you. Do not let your hearts be troubled, neither let them be afraid. [Stop allowing yourselves to be agitated and disturbed; and do not permit yourselves to be fearful and intimidated and cowardly and unsettled.]
—*John 14:27 AMP*

Don't worry about anything; instead, pray about everything. Tell God what you need, and thank him for all he has done. Then you will experience God's peace, which exceeds anything we can understand. His peace will guard your hearts and minds as you live in Christ Jesus.
—*Philippians 4:6-7 NLT*

You will keep in perfect peace all who trust in you, all whose thoughts are fixed on you!
—*Isaiah 26:3 NLT*

Day 4 HOLD UP THE SHIELD OF FAITH

*Let your **faith** be like a shield, and you will be able to stop all the flaming arrows of the evil one.*

—Ephesians 6:16 CEV

The fourth piece of armor God instructs us to use is the *shield of faith*. As said earlier, the shield rested on a small clip on the soldier's belt when not in use, showing that our faith is inseparably linked to the Word of God. If a person is not feeding on God's Word, he can have no faith.[12]

The Greek word for *shield* is *thureos*, a term for a door that was wide and tall. The shield was door-sized, completely covering a man. Every person entering the Roman army was measured for his shield to make sure it completely covered him.[13]

In most cases, the shield was made of six layers of animal hide tightly woven together and mounted on wood. It was extremely durable and practically impenetrable. A soldier would rub oil deep into the leather every morning to keep it soft and flexible. Without oil, the shield would eventually harden, crack, and break into pieces when put under pressure—proving to be deadly in the midst of combat. Before going into battle, a soldier would also soak his shield in water until it was fully saturated. In this way, if a shield was hit by an enemy's flaming arrow, the water–soaked shield would extinguish the fire.[14]

What is God showing you about faith through the Roman shield's *construction*?

_____

_____

Read Romans 12:3. How does the soldier being *measured* for his shield mirror your faith? What does this speak to you?

_____

_____

Read 1 Samuel 16:13, Jude 20, and Ephesians 5:26. What's the connection between the soldier's care of his shield—using *oil* and *water*—and your faith?

_____

_____

Can you see how vital holding up your shield of faith is? What will happen if you lay it down or fail to take care of it? *Read* 1 Timothy 1:18-19 and Hebrews 11:6.

_____

_____

For Further Study...
What comes to you through faith?
Romans 1:17; 3:21-22, 28; 5:1-2; Galatians 3:11, 14, 26; Ephesians 3:12; 2 Corinthians 5:7

Day 5 WEAR YOUR HELMET OF SALVATION

*Put on **salvation** as your helmet.*

—Ephesians 6:17 NLT

To protect our heads, God gives the *helmet of salvation*. Our minds control our lives, directly determining what comes out in our actions. Therefore, the mind must be guarded.

The soldier's bronze helmet was accented with a huge plume of brightly-colored feathers or horsehair, making a soldier very noticeable. It was decorated with engravings and covered the head from the eyebrows to about the base of the neck. Two large pieces of metal extended down the sides, protecting the cheeks, jawbone, and ears. The helmet was so strong and heavy that not even a battleaxe could pierce it. Without a helmet, the soldier would likely lose his head.[15]

What do you think it means to "take off" your helmet? Why is this dangerous?

Meditate on the message of these verses.

So brace up your minds; be sober (circumspect, morally alert); set your hope wholly and unchangeably on the grace (divine favor) that is coming to you when Jesus Christ (the Messiah) is revealed.

—1 Peter 1:13 AMP

And set your minds and keep them set on what is above (the higher things), not on the things that are on the earth.

—Colossians 3:2 AMP

And be constantly renewed in the spirit of your mind [having a fresh mental and spiritual attitude], and put on the new nature (the regenerate self) created in God's image, [Godlike] in true righteousness and holiness.

—Ephesians 4:23-24 AMP

What is the Lord speaking to you about strengthening the knowledge of your salvation?

For Further Study...

What does Scripture say about salvation? Meditate on the message of truths like these.
Psalm 27:1, 37:39; Isaiah 12:2; Acts 4:12, 13:26; Romans 1:16, 10:9-10, 13; 1 Corinthians 15:1-2; 2 Timothy 3:15-17; James 1:21; Ephesians 2:8-9

Day 6 **WIELD THE SWORD OF THE SPIRIT**

*Take the sword of the Spirit, which is the **word of God**.*

—Ephesians 6:17 NLT

It's no coincidence that God's Word is represented twice in our arsenal. The Greek term for "word" in this verse is different than the one used for the belt of truth. It's the word *rhema*, and it describes something "clearly and vividly spoken in certain, definite, undeniable terms." The Holy Spirit gives us *rhema* by making a specific verse come alive to us or supernaturally speaking to our hearts. It's a *specific*, powerful, and life-changing word with a specific purpose. Again, the *rhema* "sword" is attached to the *belt*. There is no *rhema* without the written Word.[16]

Of five different types of swords used by Roman soldiers, God picked one in particular to exemplify the sword of the Spirit. It was about 19 inches long and *double-edged*; both sides of the blade were razor sharp. When removed from the enemy's gut, the sword was twisted, causing the opponent's entrails to spill out. Of all swords, this one was most deadly.[17]

When you were in a difficult situation, did the Holy Spirit impress something on your heart? How did it arm you for what you were facing?

_____

_____

_____

When the Holy Spirit speaks a *rhema* word to our hearts, it's worth remembering. Stop and think. What are three *rhema* words that have been *milestones* in your life? How did they affect you and others?

_____

_____

_____

_____

Many believers *read* the Word; some *study* it. But the Word's *full power* is not released until it is **spoken**. When you speak against the enemy, you're lethally stabbing him with the sword of the Spirit. *Read* Revelation 1:16, 2:16; Jeremiah 23:28-29; Hebrews 4:12 and Proverbs 18:21. What is the Holy Spirit showing you about the power released when you speak the Word?

_____

_____

_____

_____

SESSION SUMMARY

Jesus suffered unfair treatment from others, and we will too. Therefore, we are to arm ourselves by remembering (1) tribulation is inevitable, (2) the troubles we face are common to all believers, and (3) we never have to lose a battle because (4) God's grace in our life is more than enough to win every battle we face. So put on the full armor of God and begin to see trials as opportunities to grow in Christ and bring Him glory!

SETTING *the* PACE

"Do not underestimate the importance of studying, meditating, and praying over the Word of God. The vital work of studying, meditating, and praying releases the Word to become a part of your own inner being. When the truth of God's Word takes root in your heart like this and begins to release its transforming power in your mind, you are then in position to confess the Word of God in a manner that will release tremendous amounts of spiritual power. This kind of confession is truly the equivalent of stabbing a two-edged sword into the heart of your adversary!"

—*Rick Renner*[18]

(1) *The Quotable Lewis*, Wayne Martindale and Jerry Root, editors (Carol Stream, IL: Tyndale House Publishers, Inc.1990) p. 587. (2) Billy Graham, *Hope for the Troubled Heart* (Nashville, TN: Thomas Nelson, 1991) pp. 79-80. (3) David Jeremiah, *Captured by Grace* (Nashville, TN: Thomas Nelson, 2006) p. 91. (4) Adapted from *Strong's Exhaustive Concordance of the Bible*, James Strong, LL.D., S.T.D. (Nashville, TN: Thomas Nelson Publishers, 1990). (5) Adapted from *Thayer's Greek-English Lexicon of the New Testament*, Joseph H. Thayer (Grand Rapids, MI: Baker Book House Company, 1977) p. 80. (6) Max Lucado, *In the Grip of Grace* (Dallas, TX: Word Publishing, 1996) pp. 132, 137. (7) Brother Lawrence, *The Practice of the Presence of God* (New Kensington, PA: Whitaker House, 1982) p. 55. (8) See note 4. (9) Adapted from *Dressed to Kill*, Rick Renner (Tulsa, OK: Teach All Nations, 2007) pp. 262, 276. (10) Ibid., pp. 292-294. (11) Ibid., pp. 313-315; 321-322. (12) Ibid., p. 343. (13) Ibid., p. 347. (14) Ibid., pp. 348-351. (15) Ibid., pp. 374-376. (16) Ibid., pp. 406-407. (17) Ibid., pp. 404-406. (18) Ibid., exact quote, p. 421.

Notes

Notes

> *As for you, my son, **be strong through the grace** that is ours in union with Christ Jesus.*
>
> **—2 Timothy 2:1 GNT**

Chapter 7

WEAPONS OF GRACE

Please refer to session 7 of the teaching series, along with chapters 9 and 10 in the Relentless book.

G 1. Grace is amazing! It is God's empowerment to live like Jesus and advance His Kingdom. To receive God's grace, we must be *submissive* to one another. Essentially, this means we're to cooperate and *come under the same mission*. Submission starts with God and extends to all others. Examine your relationships with your spouse, employer, coworkers, church leaders and members, etcetera.

Who do you find it easy to submit to? Why? What fruit is it producing?

_____

_____

_____

_____

_____

_____

_____

CORE STRENGTHENER

Another important aspect of being properly armed is having a working knowledge of the weapons we possess in Christ. Paul tells us, "The weapons we fight with are not the weapons of the world. On the contrary, they have *divine power* to demolish strongholds" (2 Corinthians 10:4 NIV). What's the "divine power" that demolishes strongholds? It's none other than God's amazing **grace**!

Who do you have difficulty submitting to? Why? What fruit is it producing?

_____

_____

_____

_____

_____

Group leader extras: James 4:7, Ephesians 5:21-24, Hebrews 13:17, 1 Peter 5:5, Romans 13:1-2.

SUBMIT

The word for *submit* and *be subject to* is the Greek word *hupotasso*. It is primarily a military term that means "to rank under" (*hupo* means "under"; *tasso* is "to arrange").[1] When we submit, we arrange ourselves or come *under* the authority of another, obeying their directions.[2] Interestingly, Webster defines *submit* as "to yield or surrender one's self and one's opinion to the power of another without murmuring."[3] Submission is at the heart of humility and is a powerful force against the enemy.

---

*All of you be submissive to one another, and be clothed with humility, for "God resists the proud, but gives **grace** to the humble." Therefore humble yourselves under the mighty hand of God, that He may exalt you in due time.*
—1 Peter 5:5-6 NKJV

2. The power to submit to each other is in God's grace, and we receive grace by *clothing ourselves with humility*. Think about getting dressed each day. It requires purposeful action; it doesn't happen automatically. Meditate on these verses and, in your own words, briefly describe what it means to *put on* humility.

> Instead, clothe yourself with the presence of the Lord Jesus Christ. And don't let yourself think about ways to indulge your evil desires.
> —*Romans 13:14 NLT*

> Let the Lord Jesus Christ be as near to you as the clothes you wear. Then you won't try to satisfy your selfish desires.
> —*Romans 13:14 CEV*

> I have been crucified with Christ: and I myself no longer live, but *Christ lives in me*. And the real life I now have within this body is a result of my trusting in the Son of God, who loved me and gave himself for me.
> —*Galatians 2:20 TLB*

> All who keep His commandments [who obey His orders and follow His plan, live and continue to live, to stay and] abide in Him, and He in them. [They let Christ be a home to them and they are the home of Christ.] And by this we know and understand and have the proof that He [really] lives and makes His home in us: by the [Holy] Spirit Whom He has given us.
> —*1 John 3:24 AMP*

HUMILITY

In Scripture, *humility* means "to have a humble opinion of one's self; a deep sense of one's (moral) littleness, modesty or lowliness of mind."[4] Webster says humility is "freedom from pride and arrogance; the act of submission."[5] To be truly humble means we believe, trust, and obey God's Word over what we think, feel, or desire.

3. *Humility* is the number one element necessary to receiving God's grace. It is *not* a quality we innately possess or can develop on our own. It is an attribute of God's grace imparted to us by Christ Himself as His Spirit lives in us and we learn to live in Him.

CORE STRENGTHENER

True humility is absolute obedience and dependence on God. It puts Him first, others second, and ourselves third in all things. Humility has nothing to do with being weak, soft-spoken, or self-demeaning, but has everything to do with living boldly, relentlessly, in the power of God's free gift of grace.

Ponder these words of and about Jesus.

Come to Me, all you who labor and are heavy-laden and overburdened, and I will cause you to rest. [I will ease and relieve and refresh your souls.] Take My yoke upon you and learn of Me, for I am gentle (meek) and *humble* (lowly) in heart, and you will find rest (relief and ease and refreshment and recreation and blessed quiet) for your souls. For My yoke is wholesome (useful, good—not harsh, hard, sharp, or pressing, but comfortable, gracious, and pleasant), and My burden is light and easy to be borne.

—*Matthew 11:28-30 AMP*

Jesus knew that he had come from God and would go back to God. He also knew that the Father had given him complete power. So during the meal Jesus got up, removed his outer garment, and wrapped a towel around his waist. He put some water into a large bowl. Then he began washing his disciples' feet and drying them with the towel he was wearing.

—*John 13:3-5 CEV*

Let this same attitude and purpose and [humble] mind be in you which was in Christ Jesus: [Let Him be your example in humility:] (AMP) Though he was God, he did not think of equality with God as something to cling to. Instead, he gave up his divine privileges; he took the humble position of a slave and was born as a human being. When he appeared in human form, he humbled himself in obedience to God and died a criminal's death on a cross. Therefore, God elevated him to the place of highest honor and gave him the name above all other names. (NLT)

—*Philippians 2:5-9*

What picture of humility is developing on the screen of your heart from these verses?

_____

_____

_____

SETTING *the* PACE

"Here we have the root and nature of true humility. ...We must learn of Jesus, how He is meek and lowly of heart. He teaches us where true humility takes its rise and finds its strength: in the knowledge that *it is God who worketh all in all, and that our place is to yield to Him in perfect resignation and dependence*—in full consent to be and to do nothing of ourselves. This is the life Christ came to reveal and to impart...for it is the indwelling Christ who will live in us this life, meek and lowly."
—*Andrew Murray*[6]

"I believe that God wants to make real to us all this ideal of humility where we so recognize human helplessness and human insufficiency that we shall rest no more on human plans and human devices and human energy, but continually look to God for His thought, for His voice, for His power, for His all-sufficiency in all things."
—*Smith Wigglesworth*[7]

4. It is very important to understand the value of true humility. Take a moment to slowly read its definition. In what areas of life do you struggle to humble yourself and trust God? Fear is often the root cause of a lack of trust. Pray and ask God to show you what you fear and why. Then surrender it to Him.

The areas in which I find it hard to trust God are...

_____

_____

_____

God is showing me I worry or fear because...

_____

_____

_____

I asked the Lord for help, and he saved me from all my fears. Keep your eyes on the Lord! You will shine like the sun and never blush with shame.
—Psalm 34:4-5 CEV

5. Pride is the opposite of humility, and no one is immune to its infectious reach—not even those close to God. Lucifer was close to God, serving as a mighty angel in His presence. But when the iniquity of pride was found in his heart, God cast him out.

Meditate on the Message of these scriptures.
These six things the Lord hates, indeed, seven are an abomination to Him: A proud look [the spirit that makes one overestimate himself and underestimate others]...
—*Proverbs 6:16-17 AMP*

You rebuke the proud—the cursed, who stray from Your commandments.
—*Psalm 119:21 NKJV*

Pride goes before destruction, a haughty spirit before a fall. Better to be lowly in spirit and among the oppressed than to share plunder with the proud.
—*Proverbs 16:18-19 NIV*

Pride leads to conflict; those who take advice are wise.
—*Proverbs 13:10 NLT*

When swelling and pride come, then emptiness and shame come also, but with the humble (those who are lowly, who have been pruned or chiseled by trial, and renounce self) are skillful and godly Wisdom and soundness.
—*Proverbs 11:2 AMP*

What is God showing you about pride—its cause, what it produces, and how it can be averted?

_____

_____

Group leader extras: Lucifer's fall is recorded in Isaiah 14:12-17 and Ezekiel 28:11-19.

PRIDE

The word *proud* means "showing one's self above others, preeminent; having an arrogant estimate of one's means or merits; despising others or treating them with contempt."[8] Synonyms include *conceited*, *smug*, and *self-righteous*. Pride manifests in lofty airs, rudeness, and impatience.

G | 6. Scripture repeatedly links *pride with unbelief* and *humility with faith*. Pause and ponder the meaning of these words. What would you say is the connection between pride and a *lack* of faith in God and between humility and faith?

The connection between pride and unbelief is...

_____

_____

_____

The connection between humility and faith is...

_____

_____

_____

CORE STRENGTHENER

Pride is very deceitful. It's the most effective weapon of darkness that keeps people from finishing well. The proud get blindsided because they can't see the enemy's advances. When we exalt our own opinion over God's, we enter pride, lose our rear guard, and our backside becomes uncovered.

SETTING *the* PACE

"There is one vice of which no man in the world is free; which everyone in the world loathes when he sees it in someone else; and of which hardly any people, except Christians ever imagine that they are guilty themselves. ...The essential vice, the utmost evil, is **Pride**. Unchastity, anger, greed, drunkenness, and all that, are mere flea-bites in comparison: it was through Pride that the devil became the devil; Pride leads to every other vice: it is the complete anti-God state of mind. ...As long as you are proud you cannot know God. A proud man is always looking down on things and people; and, of course, as long as you are looking down, you cannot see something that is above you."
—*C. S. Lewis*[9]

CORE STRENGTHENER

To be clothed in humility is to wear God's armor rather than our own. It takes genuine humility to have faith, because when you are humble, you rely on and trust in God's ability (grace) to pull you through—not your own ability.

7. Read the account of Israel's exploration of the Promised Land in Numbers 13:27-33 and 14:6-9. On what did ten of the spies focus and base their chance of victory, and why was it prideful? In contrast, on what did Joshua and Caleb focus and base their hope of victory? How was their response humble and filled with faith? What does this say to you?

The 10 spies were focused and based their chance of victory on...

_____

_____

_____

Caleb and Joshua focused and based their hope of victory on...

_____

_____

_____

This example of pride and unbelief versus humility and faith tells me...

_____

_____

_____

*There is a way that **seems** right to a man, but in the end it leads to death.*
—Proverbs 14:12 NIV

8. At all times, we are either trusting in God or in man. Trust in man includes trust in ourselves and what we can do in our own abilities. Carefully read these passages and identify the *blessings* of humbly trusting God and the *curses* of trusting in man. Which do you see manifesting more consistently in your life?

I, the Lord, have put a curse on those who turn from me and trust in human strength. They will dry up like a bush in salty desert soil, where nothing can grow. But I will bless those who trust me. They will be like trees growing beside a stream—trees with roots that reach down to the water, and with leaves that are always green. They bear fruit every year and are never worried by a lack of rain.

—*Jeremiah 17:5-8 CEV*

Trust in the LORD with all your heart; do not depend on your own understanding. Seek his will in all you do, and he will show you which path to take. Don't be impressed with your own wisdom. Instead, fear the Lord and turn away from evil. Then you will have healing for your body and strength for your bones.

—*Proverbs 3:5-8 NLT*

The *blessings* of humbly trusting God are...

_____

_____

_____

The *curses* of foolishly trusting man are (including the blessings I miss out on)...

_____

_____

_____

_____

_____

_____

Group leader extras: Proverbs 28:26, Psalm 146:3-10.

SETTING *the* PACE

"Nothing sets a person so much out of the devil's reach as *humility*."
—*Jonathan Edwards*[10]

Those who think they can do it on their own end up obsessed with measuring their own moral muscle but never get around to exercising it in real life. Those who trust God's action in them find that God's Spirit is in them—living and breathing God! Obsession with self in these matters is a dead end; attention to God leads us out into the open, into a spacious, free life. Focusing on the self is the opposite of focusing on God. Anyone completely absorbed in self ignores God, ends up thinking more about self than God. That person ignores who God is and what he is doing. And God isn't pleased at being ignored.
—Romans 8:5-8 The Message

9. How important to you is your opinion or the opinion of others? When it comes to matters of finances, health, ministry, politics, parenting, etc., who has the *final word* in your life—you, your friends, your family, or God? When someone asks for advice, what do you give them—your opinion or God's

Word? How does this session on humility challenge you?

_____

_____

_____

*Clothe (apron) yourselves, all of you, with humility [as the garb of a servant, so that its covering cannot possibly be stripped from you, with freedom from pride and arrogance] toward one another. For **God sets Himself against the proud** (the insolent, the overbearing, the disdainful, the presumptuous, the boastful)—[and He opposes, frustrates, and defeats them], but gives grace (favor, blessing) to the humble.*
—1 Peter 5:5 AMP

10. Scripture states that God *opposes* and *frustrates* the proud. Are you in a situation in which it seems you have hit a brick wall—you want to move forward but can't? If so, humble yourself before God and pray. Ask Him to show you your heart in the situation. If He reveals an attitude of pride within you, He Himself may be opposing you. Repent and ask Him for wisdom and grace to respond in humility. Write anything He reveals.

_____

_____

_____

Sample Prayer

Father, I ask You to forgive me for walking in pride. Forgive me for being rude and impatient with others. Thank You for Your mercy and forgiveness and for a better understanding of humility. Continue to expand my understanding and develop this treasured virtue within me. Help me to say every day that "I" no longer live but that You, Jesus, live in me by the power of Your Spirit. Give me the grace to submit to those I am in relationship with. Help me to trust You fully and not to lean on my own understanding. I don't want to be phony; I want to be real. I love You, Father. In Jesus' name, Amen.

Weekly
CHALLENGE

We have all already experienced miracles in our lives, the greatest of which is our redemption from sin and death. Remembering the work of God enables us to remain humbly dependent on His grace when difficulties arise. This week, share the testimony of what God has done for you with at least three different people. Your story will encourage your brothers and sisters in the faith and draw those far from God to Him, and you will be strengthened in your spirit as you recall His work in your life.

Day 1 **HUMILITY IS TRUSTING GOD**

I will remove all proud and arrogant people from among you. ...Those who are left will be the lowly and **humble***, for* **it is they who trust in the name of the Lord***.*
—Zephaniah 3:11-12 NLT

Faith and trust are one and the same. Faith is trusting God. Everything—I mean everything—we receive from God comes through faith. Because of His incomprehensible love, He sent Jesus to die in our place and pay for our sins so that we could be restored to a right relationship with Him forever. That's the Gospel in a nutshell—John 3:16. But in order to receive this priceless gift, we must *believe* what He says in His Word is true. That's trust. It all boils down to trust.

TRUST

To *trust* is to "place confidence in; to rely or rest the mind on the integrity, veracity, justice, friendship, or sound principle of another person."[11] When we trust God, we take Him at His Word. Synonyms for trust include *have faith in, believe, rely on, depend on, expect, hope, count on,* and *be sure about.*

The Bible defines faith in Colossians 1:4: "For we have heard of your **faith** in Christ Jesus [*the leaning of your entire human personality on Him in* **absolute** **trust** *and confidence in His power, wisdom, and goodness*]...." (AMP).

God is worthy of your trust! Have you blamed God for things that you now realize were attacks from the enemy? Name some things you trusted God for in the past that He provided. Meditate on His faithfulness!

_____

_____

_____

_____

Personal experiences that don't line up with Scripture can become huge barriers to trusting God. Is there an experience you or someone close to you has had that is trying to trump God's truth? What is it and what scriptures can you find to strengthen your faith and refute the argument?

_____

_____

_____

_____

CORE STRENGTHENER

In Scripture, the *hand of God* always speaks of His ability, power, might, or strength; it's His armor. Practically speaking, we are to humble ourselves under God's might and strength, refusing to allow our own human ideas and experiences (ours and others) to rise above the Word of God. Instead, we *believe* God's Word, regardless of our natural reason or logic, and allow it to dictate our actions.

Day 2 HUMILITY IS THE FEAR OF THE LORD

True humility and fear of the Lord lead to riches, honor, and long life.
—**Proverbs 22:4 NLT**

Fearing the Lord does *not* mean to be afraid of Him. It means honoring and reverencing Him in awe of all that He is. It is greatly admiring and respecting Him, knowing that He is everything He says He is and will do everything He says He'll do. As Solomon declared, "Fear-of-GOD is a school in skilled living—first you learn humility, then you experience glory" (Proverbs 15:33, The Message).

When we fear the Lord, we have no other "gods" before Him—He holds the highest place of honor in our lives. When we fear God, we seek first His Kingdom and give Him the first fruits of our income. We are willing to extend mercy and forgiveness to others, and we desire to please Him in all our ways. If we sin, we don't run from Him; we run to Him to get things right between us. Indeed, the fear of the Lord is the beginning of wisdom!

SETTING *the* PACE

"Fearing God is *not* a developmental phase we pass through. The fear of the Lord is a permanent part of our walk with God, fervently springing from hearts that yearn to be near God and to be like Him."
—*Neil T. Anderson and Rich Miller*[12]

In your own words, explain how the fear of the Lord is inseparably linked to humility. How does pride reveal a lack of godly fear?

_____

_____

_____

Meditate on Psalm 34:11-14, Deuteronomy 10:12-13, and Proverbs 8:13. How do these scriptures help you better understand the fear of the Lord?

_____

_____

Slowly read Psalm 104, 147:4-5 and Isaiah 40:12, 66:1-2. How does pondering God's greatness humble you and instill reverential fear in you?

_____

_____

For Further Study...
The Blessings of Fearing the Lord
Psalm 25:12-14, 31:19, 33:18-19, 34:7-10, 103:11-13, 112:1-3, 115:11-13, 128:1-4, 145:19
Proverbs 10:27, 14:26-27

For more on this topic, see John's curriculum **The Fear of the Lord.**

Day 3 HUMILITY IS WALKING IN LOVE

And walk in love, [esteeming and delighting in one another] as Christ loved us.
—Ephesians 5:2 AMP

Nothing is sweeter to our heavenly Father than to see His children *walk* in *love*. Of all the fruit of the Spirit, love holds the highest place. God's love demonstrated through Christ is true humility. Before going to the cross, Jesus told us to "love one another" four times in less than twenty-four hours. Clearly it's important.

Every godly attribute grows from God's love. We need love to be kind and patient, to forgive others and pursue peace. Without love there is no salvation or righteousness in Christ. This makes sense when we realize that **God is love** (see 1 John 4:8). It is not just something He does. It's who He is.

What does love look like? First Corinthians 13:4-8 (AMP) gives us a powerful portait. Slowly read this passage:

Love endures long and is patient and kind; love never is envious nor boils over with jealousy, is not boastful or vainglorious, does not display itself haughtily.

It is not conceited (arrogant and inflated with pride); it is not rude (unmannerly) and does not act unbecomingly. Love (God's love in us) does not insist on its own rights or its own way, for it is not self-seeking; it is not touchy or fretful or resentful; it takes no account of the evil done to it [it pays no attention to a suffered wrong]. It does not rejoice at injustice and unrighteousness, but rejoices when right and truth prevail.

Love bears up under anything and everything that comes, is ever ready to believe the best of every person, its hopes are fadeless under all circumstances, and it endures everything [without weakening]. Love never fails [never fades out or becomes obsolete or comes to an end].

In what ways are love and humility related? How is love the opposite of pride?

_____

_____

_____

God loves us and gives us *His* love so we can love others (see Romans 5:5; 1 John 4:19). Read 1 Thessalonians 3:12 and 1 John 4:12, 16-17 and describe how His love *grows* in us.

_____

_____

_____

_____

_____

SETTING *the* PACE

"Love is a fruit, in season at all times and within the reach of every hand. Anyone may gather it and no limit is set."
—Mother Teresa[13]

Day 4 HUMILITY IS PURSUING PEACE

*If possible, as far as it depends on you, **live at peace** with everyone.*
—Romans 12:18 AMP

God has given us shoes of peace as part of our armor. We are to stand firm and walk in peace everywhere we go. God says, "Search for peace (harmony; undisturbedness from fears, agitating passions, and moral conflicts) and seek it eagerly. [Do not merely desire peaceful relations with God, with your fellowmen, and with yourself, but *pursue, go after them*!]" (1 Peter 3:11 AMP) Peace produces unity and releases God's power. While pride wants its own way and only cares about self, peace thinks of God first, others second, and self last.

Carefully consider this peace-promoting wisdom.

> Don't think you are better than you really are. Be honest in your evaluation of yourselves, measuring yourselves by the faith God has given us.
> —*Romans 12:3 NLT*

> Live in harmony with one another; do not be haughty (snobbish, high-minded, exclusive), but readily adjust yourself to [people, things] and give yourselves to humble tasks. Never overestimate yourself or be wise in your own conceits.
> —*Romans 12:16 AMP*

> I beg you to live in a way that is worthy of the people God has chosen to be his own. Always be humble and gentle. Patiently put up with each other and love each other. Try your best to let God's Spirit keep your hearts united. Do this by living at peace.
> —*Ephesians 4:1-3 CEV*

What major principles of humility are recurring in these verses?

_____

_____

Read Jesus' words in Matthew 6:14-15 and Mark 11:25-26. What indispensable principle of peace is revealed? How does this relate to humility?

_____

_____

Is there someone you're struggling to live at peace with? Take the situation to God and release it in prayer. Ask Him to forgive you for holding on to any unforgiveness, and pray a blessing over their life. Do this as often as the negative thoughts and feelings return. In time, they will cease.

For Further Study...
Encouragement to live in unity:
1 Corinthians 1:10; 2 Corinthians 13:11; Philippians 1:27; 1 Peter 3:8-12

Day 5 HUMILITY IS SELFLESSNESS

*Then Jesus said to the disciples, "If any of you wants to be my follower, **you must put aside your selfish ambition**, shoulder your cross, and follow me.*
—Matthew 16:24-25 NLT

Humility equals selflessness. Jesus Christ was the embodiment of both. From the time He left heaven until the time He returned, His life remained focused on one thing: to do the will of the Father. Again and again, Scripture records Jesus saying things like, "I have come down from heaven not to do my will but to do the will of him who sent me" (John 6:38 NIV).

Jesus had one task—one focus—that compelled Him to do the will of the Father even to the point of death. May we each learn to live humbly and bring glory to the Father in all we do.

Meditate on the message of this amazing declaration.

I am able to do nothing from Myself [independently, of My own accord—but only as I am taught by God and as I get His orders]. Even as I hear, I judge [I decide as I am bidden to decide. As the voice comes to Me, so I give a decision], and My judgment is right (just, righteous), because I do not seek or consult My own will [I have no desire to do what is pleasing to Myself, My own aim, My own purpose] but only the will and pleasure of the Father Who sent Me.

—John 5:30 AMP

Ask yourself these questions and answer honestly:

What's driving my life? What motivates me to get out of bed every morning and do what I do?

_____

_____

_____

Am I living selfishly or selflessly? What evidence is there to back up my answer?

_____

_____

_____

Am I eternally impacting others? If so, how? If not, what can I do to change that?

_____

_____

_____

Get quiet before the Lord and ask Him for His insight. He loves you so much and desires to give you a fulfilling life beyond your wildest dreams!

Day 6 HUMILITY IS TOTAL DEPENDENCE ON GOD

*I am the vine. You are the branches. Those who live in me while I live in them will produce a lot of fruit. But **you can't produce anything without me**.*
—John 15:5 GW

A newborn cradled in her mother's arms is helpless. She cries for food, unable to feed herself. She cries to be cleaned. She cries to be warmed and cries to be comforted. What a picture of total dependence. In a similar way, we are dependent on God. Though we mature and learn to advance God's kingdom, we remain reliant on Him. Why? So that we will remain humble.

For in Him we live and move and have our being.
—Acts 17:28 AMP

Meditate on the message of these verses.

We [Christians]...put no confidence or dependence [on what we are] in the flesh and on outward privileges and physical advantages and external appearances.
—*Philippians 3:3 AMP*

For I know that nothing good dwells...In my flesh. I can will what is right, but I cannot perform it.
—*Romans 7:18 AMP*

It is the Spirit Who gives life [He is the Life-giver]; the flesh conveys no benefit whatever [there is no profit in it]. The words (truths) that I have been speaking to you are spirit and life.
—*John 6:63 AMP*

What humbling perspective is God revealing to you about your flesh? How does Philippians 4:13 bring balance and encouragement?

_____

_____

SETTING *the* PACE

"Our lives, we are told, are but fleeting at best, like roses they fade and decay; then let us do good while the present is ours, be useful as long as we stay."
—*Fanny Crosby*[14]

Are you in a situation that is reminding you of your total dependence on God? If so, briefly describe how it is challenging you. Then get quiet before the Lord. Ask Him to strengthen you with His grace and give you a glimpse of the glory He is developing in you.

_____

_____

_____

SESSION SUMMARY

As a child of God, you are in a war. But He has armed you with weapons of grace. Humility is one of those weapons. It arms you to live relentlessly. By clothing yourself with humility—allowing Jesus Christ to live His life through you—you position yourself to receive the empowerment of God's grace.

Notes

(1) Adapted from *Vine's Complete Expository Dictionary of Old and New Testament Words*, W.E. Vine (Nashville, TN: Thomas Nelson Publishing, 1996) p. 606. (2) Adapted from *Thayer's Greek-English Lexicon of the New Testament*, Joseph H. Thayer (Grand Rapids, MI: Baker Book House Company, 1977) p. 645. (3) Adapted from *Noah Webster's First Edition of an American Dictionary of the English Language* (1828), Republished in facsimile edition by Foundation for American Christian Education (San Francisco, CA 2000). (4) See note 2, p. 614. (5) See note 3. (6) *Andrew Murray*, Humility (Fort Washington, PA: CLC Publications, 1997) p. 28. (7) Smith Wigglesworth, *Faith That Prevails* (Springfield, MO: Gospel Publishing House, 1966) p. 50. (8) See note 2, p. 641. (9) Quotes by *C. S. Lewis* (retrieved 8/13/11, http://dailychristianquote.com/dcqpride.html). (10) Christian quotes on *Pride and Humility* (retrieved 7/23/11, http://dailychristianquote.com/dcqpride.html). (11) See note 3. (12) Neil T. Anderson & Rich Miller, *Freedom from Fear* (Eugene, OR: Harvest House Publishers, 1999) p. 261. (13) Mother Teresa, *No Greater Love* (Novato, CA: New World Library, 2001) p. 22. (14) *Fast Break, Five-Minute Devotions to Start Your Day* (St. San Luis Obispo, CA: Parable, 2007) Day 342.

*Therefore, since we are surrounded by such a huge crowd of witnesses to the life of faith, **let us strip off every weight that slows us down**, especially the sin that so easily trips us up. And let us run with endurance the race God has set before us.*

—Hebrews 12:1 NLT

8

THROW OFF THE WEIGHT

Please refer to session 8 of the teaching series,
along with chapter 11 in the Relentless book.

1. Our Christian life is like running a marathon race. In order to keep a steady pace and go the distance, we have to *throw off* every unnecessary weight. Stop and think. What needless activities, attitudes, relationships, or ways of thinking are hindering or endangering your progress in Christ? What is the Holy Spirit pointing out to you, and what action(s) is He prompting you to take?

   The **unnecessary weights** the Holy Spirit is showing me are...

   _____
   _____
   _____

   Think: What is *distracting* you, *stealing your time*, and *getting your focus* off God and what He has called you to do?

   The **plan of action** He wants me to take to throw off these weights is...

   _____
   _____

   Think: How can you eliminate these things, lighten your load, and strengthen your spirit to press toward the finish line?

2. God also wants us to throw off every *sin* that easily entangles and trips us up. Stop and think. What sin(s) do you easily fall into? Is it impure thinking or worry and fear? Is it gossip or being easily offended? Ask the Lord to

CORE STRENGTHENER

It's a fact verified again and again throughout God's Word: If you are going to fulfill your God-planned journey, you'll need to leave the weight of your cares and concerns with Him. His path often goes against what dictates security and comfort, and yet it is one of adventure, faith, and great reward.

SETTING *the* PACE

"Lay aside all inordinate affection and concern for the body, and the present life and world. Inordinate [*excessive*] care for the present life, or fondness of it, is a dead weight upon the soul that pulls it down when it should ascend upwards, and pulls it back when it should press forward; it makes duty and difficulties harder, and heavier than they would be."
—*Matthew Henry*[1]
[Italicized word in brackets added for clarity.]

show you what it is, why you are easily ensnared, and how to avoid it.

The sin(s) that easily entangles me is...

_____

_____

The reason I'm easily ensnared and how I can avoid entanglement is...

_____

_____

_____

*Therefore humble yourselves [demote, lower yourselves in your own estimation] under the mighty hand of God, that in due time He may exalt you, **casting the whole of your care** [all your anxieties, all your worries, all your concerns, once and for all] on Him, for He cares for you affectionately and cares about you watchfully.*
—1 Peter 5:6-7 AMP

3. Sometimes the unnecessary weights overloading us are the *cares* of life. These are whatever causes anxiety, worry, doubt, or fear. What tends to weigh you down, choking the life of Christ within you and stealing your peace, joy, patience, and self-control?

The **cares** that choke the life of Christ in me and weigh me down are...

_____

_____

_____

Now pray aloud, cast your cares on Jesus, and receive His peace. Ask for grace to trust Him to care for everything and to focus on the tasks He's called you to do. Do this until you feel the weight is truly gone.

"CASTING YOUR CARES"

The word *casting* is taken from the Greek word *epiripto*, which is a compounding of *epi* and *ripto*. *Epi* means "upon or on top of something"; *ripto* means "to hurl, throw, or cast," and it often meant to do it "violently or with great force." In secular literature, the use of this word often pictured a traveler hurling a garment, bag, or excess weight from off his shoulders onto the back of a beast of burden, such as a camel, donkey, or horse.

The word *cares* is the Greek word *merimna*, which means "anxiety." This describes any trouble, affliction, difficulty, hardship, or complicated circumstance that arises in our lives. In essence, *casting your cares* means "to forcefully throw anything that's causing you anxiety or worry onto the shoulders of Jesus and let Him bear it." Why? Because He cares for you![2]

G 4. Jesus does *not* want us to worry, not even about the legitimate needs for our family or ourselves. Instead He wants us to *cast our cares* on Him. The act of casting our cares is a sign of humility. Trying to figure everything out and provide for ourselves is a sign of pride. Carefully read Matthew 6:25-34. What is the Lord speaking to you about not worrying?

_____

_____

_____

_____

5. God has a specific "race course" marked out just for you. It is linked to the burning desire He has placed in your heart. What do you feel God is calling you to do? How has He confirmed it? How are you cooperating with Him to bring it about?

_____

_____

_____

_____

_____

I trust in you, O Lord; I say, "You are my God."
My times are in your hands; deliver me from
my enemies and from those who pursue me.
Let your face shine on your servant;
save me in your unfailing love.
—Psalm 31:14-16 NIV

G 6. When God speaks something to our heart and its manifestation is delayed, we sometimes try to *help God* bring it about. This too is a care we must cast on Him because our times are in His hands. Are you trying to help God and

SETTING *the* PACE

"It is not part of God's plan for you to lie awake at night, tossing and turning and wondering, *How am I going to pay my bills if I lose my job? What am I going to do when I retire if the stock market continues to decline? How am I going to provide for my family if my company goes through bankruptcy?* or any concern that you may have. ... From cover to cover, the Bible has a clear message that God is the One who provides for all your needs. No need is too massive, too problematic, or too severe for Jesus to meet it!"
—Charles Stanley[3]

achieve your destiny in your ability? What can you learn from Abraham and Sarah's example to apply in your life? (See Genesis 16, 21:8-13 and Galatians 4:22-31.)

_____

_____

_____

SETTING _the_ PACE

"The flesh can also get religious and try to _help God out_. Abraham and Sarah are a great illustration of this during the years they waited for God to fulfill His promise and give them a child. ... The motives of Abraham and Sarah were good. But please take note that even when you use the flesh to try to do something good, God rejects it."
—Tony Evans[4]

CORE STRENGTHENER

At various times in our lives, each of us has to choose between _security_ and _destiny_. Will we choose the path leading to significance or attempt to secure our well-being? If you choose the course of self-preservation, its end will not be your divine destiny. You may succeed in maintaining your comfort and security, but you'll eventually discover the fullness of life you forfeited at the judgment seat of Christ.

7. Being ready to do what you believe God is calling you to do is important, but _not_ serving anywhere until the perfect opportunity arises is unwise. What opportunities has God placed in front of you? Are you serving Him in any of them? If not, why? What are you waiting for?

_____

_____

_____

> If you wait for perfect conditions,
> you will never get anything done.
> —Eccleslastes 11:4 TLB

8. When we obediently step out on God's Word, we experience His miraculous provision. Describe three occasions when God came through for you. How do these memories keep your faith alive and your heart tender toward Him?

God came through when

_____

_____

_____

God came through when

_____

_____

_____

God came through when

_____

_____

_____

God is faithful (reliable, trustworthy, and therefore ever true to His promise, and He can be depended on); by Him you were called into companionship and participation with His Son, Jesus Christ our Lord.
—1 Corinthians 1:9 AMP

9. Have you come under attack doing what God has called you to do? Lift up your shield of faith and wield the sword of the Spirit. Pray and ask the Holy Spirit to recall specific scriptures (*rhema* words) He has made alive to you that fit your present situation. *Write* them and *speak* them aloud over your life and against the enemy.

The **rhema words** the Holy Spirit has spoken to me include...

_____

_____

_____

_____

_____

_____

_____

10. When trouble hits, God does *not* want you to worry, panic, or complain. Instead of reacting negatively out of instinct, He wants you to purposely *act* in a positive way, believing Him for victory in the situation.

Meditate on the message of these verses. Let them become the wallpaper of your mind.

Don't worry about anything; instead, pray about everything. Tell God what you need, and thank him for all he has done. If you do this, you will experience God's peace, which is far more

---

SETTING *the* PACE

"[God] is faithful in His love. ...He is faithful to His purpose; He does not begin a work and then leave it undone. He is faithful to His relationships. As a Father He will not renounce His children; as a Friend He will not deny His people; as a Creator He will not forsake the work of His own hands. He is faithful to His promises and will never allow one of them to fail for a single believer."
—***Charles H. Spurgeon***[5]
[Word in brackets added for clarity.]

SETTING *the* PACE

"Romans 10:17 shows us that the material used to build faith is more than just reading God's Word: 'Faith comes by hearing, and hearing by the Word of God.' In this scripture 'word' is not logos, but *rhema*. Faith specifically comes by hearing the *rhema*. ...If for no other reason, you should carefully study the Bible—Genesis to Revelation—in order to give the Holy Spirit the material with which He needs to work. Then when you wait upon the Lord, the Holy Spirit will impart His faith to you."
—***Dr. Paul Yonggi Cho***[6]

wonderful than the human mind can understand. His peace will guard your hearts and minds as you live in Christ Jesus. And now, dear brothers and sisters, let me say one more thing as I close this letter. Fix your thoughts on what is true and honorable and right. Think about things that are pure and lovely and admirable. Think about things that are excellent and worthy of praise.

—*Philippians 4:6-8 NLT*

Steep your life in God-reality, God-initiative, God-provisions. Don't worry about missing out. You'll find all your everyday human concerns will be met. Give your entire attention to what God is doing right now, and don't get worked up about what may or may not happen tomorrow. God will help you deal with whatever hard things come up when the time comes.

—*Matthew 6:33-34 The Message*

What new response can you develop from these verses in exchange for worry and fear?

_____

_____

_____

_____

CORE STRENGTHENER

Our Father knows the best training course for each of us, and though He doesn't author the hardships, He permits them in order to strengthen us for the destiny before us. *Don't circumvent your training process.* The trials you face today are preparing you for the great feats you'll accomplish tomorrow!

Weekly CHALLENGE

The Holy Spirit knows better than you do how to build faith in your life. He alone can train you to choose destiny over security so that you can walk in greater kingdom authority. Spend time in prayer this week to ask the Holy Spirit how he would train you to cast your cares on Him. He may ask you to increase your regular giving to your church, become a partner with a ministry, sponsor a child in another country, or give a spontaneous gift to someone. When these actions are prompted by divine direction, you will have an unshakeable foundation to act in faith regardless of any circumstances.

Day 1 **GUARD YOUR HEART**

*Above all else, guard your heart, for **it affects everything** you do.*
—Proverbs 4:23 NLT

When we obediently follow God's Word, we are often attacked by the enemy. One attack we sometimes face is the temptation to be offended with God. We often develop expectations of *how* and *when* He is going to do things. When our expectations are not met, we become disappointed. And "unrelenting disappointment leaves you heartsick" (Proverbs 13:12 The Message).

If we don't throw off the disappointment and surrender it to God, it can deepen and create a wound in our soul. This happened to one of the greatest men in history, John the Baptist. He loved God and was sold out to Him, but when he found himself imprisoned, his faith was severely shaken.

Carefully read Matthew 11:2-6. Compare John's question in verse 3 with John 1:29-36. What might be a reason for his change in thinking? Have you experienced this?

_____

_____

_____

In reply to John, Jesus reported the miracles taking place and that the Gospel was being preached. He then said, "And blessed is the one who is not offended by me" (Matthew 11:6 ESV). What do these words from Jesus speak to you?

_____

_____

_____

Therefore I always exercise and discipline myself...to have a clear
*(unshaken, blameless) conscience, **void of offense** toward God.*
—Acts 24:16 AMP

Do you struggle to understand why God allowed certain things to happen in your life? Are you upset with Him? If so, pray. Tell Him how you feel. Ask Him to give you grace to trust Him in the situation and continue to be relentless. Take some time to wait in His presence. Receive His love and acceptance. Write anything He speaks to your heart.

_____

_____

_____

_____

Day 2 YOU'RE GROWING FROM FAITH TO FAITH

*For I am not ashamed of the gospel of Christ, for it is the power of God to salvation for everyone who believes. ...For in it the righteousness of God is revealed from **faith to faith**; as it is written, "The just shall live by faith."*
—Romans 1:16-17 NKJV

Growth in God is gradual, like a child's progression in through school. He doesn't start in tenth grade when he is five. He starts out on the level of development he can handle. As he masters the material, he is tested. Once he passes all the tests for the level he can, he is promoted to the next. That's what Paul means when he says the righteousness of God is revealed in us from *faith* to *faith*.

Notice that our growth from faith to faith is directly linked with the gospel. The Word is the textbook of all textbooks, and our primary teacher is the Holy Spirit. He always knows exactly what we need and how to administer the necessary tests to equip us for what's ahead.

Faith building is a lot like bodybuilding. In bodybuilding, high repetitions of light weight produce lean muscle and strength. Low repetitions of heavy weight produce muscle growth. What does this speak to you spiritually?

_____

_____

Who is the Lord using in your life to coach, train, and support you spiritually? What are they doing that is helping you press on relentlessly?

_____

_____

In what ways has your personal trainer, the Holy Spirit, pushed you to "max out"? How have you grown spiritually as a result?

_____

_____

The Holy Spirit sees strength in you that you cannot see in yourself. Take time to thank Him for His patience, kindness, and infinite wisdom and for the spiritual muscle He is helping you build.

God keeps his promise, and he will not allow you to be tested beyond your power to remain firm; at the time you are put to the test, he will give you the strength to endure it, and so provide you with a way out.
—1 Corinthians 10:13 TEV

Day 3 FIX YOUR EYES ON JESUS

Let us fix our eyes on Jesus, the author and perfecter of our faith....
—Hebrews 12:2 NIV

Right after we are instructed to "throw off" every unnecessary weight and sin, we are told to *fix our eyes on Jesus.* This is a great instruction. Think about it. What happens to you when you fix your eyes on a problem? That's right. It grows. Where our attention goes, the power flows.

The same thing happens when we fix our eyes on Jesus. When we focus our attention on all that He is—His deep love, kindness, humility, wisdom, power, and authority—all that He is grows in us. This is what David encouraged in Psalm 34:3: "O **magnify the Lord** with me, and let us exalt His name together!" (AMP)

What is the connection between throwing off weights and fixing your eyes on Jesus?

Related Scriptures: Psalm 34:5, 105:4; 2 Corinthians 3:16-18.

Read Numbers 14:21-38 and consider the outcome of the men who spied out the land.

What happened to the 10 men who fixed their eyes on their own abilities and did not trust God? (Verses 36-37.) What did their families inherit? (Verses 28-34.)

What happened to Caleb and Joshua, who fixed their eyes on God? Their families? (See Numbers 14:38 and Joshua 14:6-15, 19:49-50.)

How does this example challenge and speak to you personally?

Get quiet before the Lord. Ask Him to show you ways to fix your eyes on Jesus.

When one turns to the Lord, the veil is taken away. But we all, with unveiled face, beholding as in a mirror the glory of the Lord, are being transformed into the same image from glory to glory, just as by the Spirit of the Lord.
—2 Corinthians 3:16, 18 NKJV

Day 4 IN EVERYTHING GIVE THANKS

Thank [God] in everything [no matter what the circumstances may be, be thankful and give thanks], for this is the will of God for you [who are] in Christ Jesus....
—1 Thessalonians 5:18 AMP

Giving God thanks is powerful! It's not something we do once a year. It's something we do *every day*. Thankfulness is one of the best ways to cast our cares on God. It gets our attention onto Jesus. It helps us focus on the solution instead of the problem.

The original Greek word for *thanks* used in virtually every New Testament occurence is *eucharistia*. It's derived from *charis*, the Greek word for **grace**.[7] This tells us that the ability to give thanks in all circumstances comes from the empowerment of God's grace. It is not an act of willpower but of God-power.

Read the first two verses of Psalms 105, 106, 107, 118, and 136. What does the recurring cry of the psalmist say to you?

_____

_____

When others genuinely express thanks and appreciation to you, how does it make you feel? What does it make you want to do for them? What about when people are ungrateful?

_____

_____

_____

How do you think God feels when we genuinely express thanks and appreciation to Him?

_____

_____

Enter into His gates with thanksgiving and a thank offering and into His courts with praise! Be thankful and say so to Him, bless and affectionately praise His name! For the Lord is good; His mercy and loving-kindness are everlasting, His faithfulness and truth endure to all generations.
—Psalm 100:4-5 AMP

Create a list of at least 25 things for which you are thankful. Once your list is complete, slowly reread it, taking time to thank God for each blessing.

This is a great exercise to complete daily or anytime you begin to compare or compete with others. We truly have much to be thankful for.

For Further Study...
Ephesians 5:2,; Philippians 4:6; Colossians 3:15, 17; Hebrews 13:15; 1 Timothy 4:4

Day 5 THE JOY OF THE LORD IS YOUR STRENGTH

And be not grieved and depressed, for the joy of the Lord is your strength and stronghold.

—Nehemiah 8:10 AMP

The *joy of the Lord* is not the joy of the world, something based on or produced by circumstances. The joy of the Lord is just that—the *Lord's joy*. The Greek word for joy is *chara*, and like the word *thanks*, it is taken from *charis*, the Greek term for **grace**.[8] Joy is a supernatural aspect of God's grace, unshakable and unlimited.

> *For the kingdom of God is not a matter of eating and drinking,*
> *but of righteousness, peace and **joy in the Holy Spirit**.*
> —Romans 14:17 NIV

In John 15:11 (AMP), Jesus says, "I have told you these things, that **My joy** and delight may be in you, and that your joy and gladness may be of full measure and complete and overflowing." *Read* John 15:1-10 and identify the "things" Jesus told the disciples that release His joy.

_____

_____

Related Scripture: John 16:23-24

According to Scripture, where does joy come from, how do you receive it, and how do you stay filled with it? *Read* Psalm 4:6-7, 16:8-11, 43:4; Romans 15:13 and Galatians 5:22.

The joy of the Lord *comes from*...

_____

I *receive* the joy of the Lord by...

_____

I *remain filled* with the joy of the Lord as I...

_____

We are told to *rejoice in the Lord always* (see Philippians 4:4). What gives you reason to rejoice?

_____

_____

Related Scriptures: Psalm 5:11, 37:4; Isaiah 61:10; Luke 10:20; 1 Peter 4:12-13.

Day 6 IT'S OKAY TO LAUGH

A cheerful heart is good medicine.

—Proverbs 17:22 NIV

Laughter is one of the best medicines a person can take. It's free, has no negative side effects, and it improves your health physically, emotionally, mentally and spiritually. **Don Colbert, MD**, offers this eye-opening insight on the power of laughter:

> "In one researcher's words, laughter is like 'internal jogging.' As with aerobic exercise, laughter temporarily accelerates the heart rate, increases blood pressure and breathing, enlarges circulation and enhances the flow of oxygen in and out of the body. A hearty belly laugh also exercises the upper torso, lungs, heart, shoulders, arms, abdomen, diaphragm and legs. ...Ten belly laughs are roughly equivalent to thirty minutes of aerobic exercise.
>
> ...Laughter actually boosts the immune system and reduces harmful stress hormones in the body. In one study, there were sixteen men who watched a funny video that brought about much laughter. After a good belly laugh, the stress hormone levels of cortisol in these men decreased 39 percent and adrenaline levels fell 70 percent. At the same time, the 'feel-good' hormone endorphin rose 27 percent and the growth hormone (also known as the 'youth hormone') levels shot up 87 percent."[9]

God declares in Ecclesiastes 3:4 that there is *a time to laugh*. In Proverbs, He says, "A happy heart makes the face cheerful" and "he who has a glad heart has a continual feast [regardless of circumstances]" (15:13 NIV, 15:15 AMP). Indeed, a merry heart is good medicine!

Who makes you laugh? Whose humor or personality lifts your spirit?

_____

What clean movies, books, cartoons, etc., make you laugh? How can you ensure you get a daily dose of merriment?

_____

Learn to laugh every day. Look for appropriate opportunities to let loose. Laughter will lighten your load and improve your overall health. It's just what the doctor ordered!

Did you know? Laughter...
Reduces Stress • Lowers Blood Pressure • Boosts the Immune System • Improves Brain Function • Protects the Heart • Fosters Instant Relaxation • Connects You to Others[10]

SESSION SUMMARY

To live relentlessly, you must throw off every sin or unnecessary weight. Unnecessary weights can be attitudes, activities, ways of thinking, or the cares of life. God wants you to cast your cares onto Jesus. He wants you to be filled with His peace and joy, not anxiety, worry, or fear. Throwing off the weight is not a once-in-a-lifetime event but an ongoing process we accomplish by God's grace.

Notes

_____

(1) *The Matthew Henry Study Bible KJV*, A. Kenneth Abraham, General Editor (World Bible Publishers, Inc., 1994) p. 2601. (2) Adapted from *Sparkling Gems from the Greek*, Rick Renner (Tulsa, OK: Teach All Nations, 2003) p. 325. (3) Charles Stanley, *Finding Peace* (Nashville, TN: Thomas Nelson, Inc., 2003) p. 48. (4) Tony Evans, *Free at Last* (Chicago, IL: Moody Publishers, 2001) p. 104. (5) Charles H. Spurgeon, *All of Grace* (New Kensington, PA: Whitaker House, 1981) p. 160. (6) Dr. Paul Yonggi Cho, *The Fourth Dimension* (Plainfield, NJ: Logos International, 1979) pp. 91, 113. (7) Adapted from *The New Unger's Bible Dictionary*, Merrill F. Unger (Chicago, IL: Moody Press, 1988) p. 1271. (8) See note 2, pp. 528-529. (9) *The Miraculous Medicine of Laughter*, by Don Colbert, M.D. (*Enjoying Everyday Life*, volume 19, number 11, Nov. 2005: Joyce Meyer Ministries, Inc., Fenton, MO) p. 22. (10) Adapted from *The Seven Pillars of Health*, Don Colbert, M.D. (Lake Mary, FL: Siloam, A Strang Company, 2007) p. 246.

> *Be sober, be vigilant; because your adversary the devil walks about like a roaring lion, seeking whom he may devour.* **Resist him**, *steadfast in the faith.*

—1 Peter 5:8-9 NKJV

Chapter 9

RESIST THE DEVIL

Please refer to session 9 of the teaching series, along with chapters 12 and 13 in the Relentless book.

RESIST

The word *resist* is the Greek word *anthistemi*. It means "to stand against, oppose or withstand."[1] It implies a person who is fiercely opposed to something and is deeply determined to do everything within his power to stand against it and defy its operation.[2] Definitions for resist include *refuse to give in*, *refuse to go along with*, and *refuse to accept*.

---

*Behold! I have given **you** authority and power to trample upon serpents and scorpions, and [physical and mental strength and ability] over all the power that the enemy [possesses]; and nothing shall in any way harm you.*
—Luke 10:19 AMP

G 1. It is vital to realize that God has called and equipped *you* to fight the enemy directly. He has given *you* all power and authority to fiercely stand against Satan and his forces.

Carefully read these passages.

Be strong in the Lord [be empowered through your union with Him]; draw your strength from Him; [that strength which His boundless might provides]. Put on God's whole armor [the armor of a heavy-armed soldier which God supplies], that you may be able successfully to stand up against [all] the strategies and the deceits of the devil. For we are not wrestling with flesh and blood [contending only with physical opponents], but against the despotisms, against the powers, against [the master spirits who are] the world rulers of this present darkness, against the spirit forces of wickedness in the heavenly (supernatural) sphere. Therefore put on God's complete armor, that you may be able to resist and stand your ground on the evil day [of danger], and, having done all [the crisis demands], to stand [firmly in your place].

—*Ephesians 6:10-13 AMP*

Fight the good fight for the true faith. Hold tightly to the eternal life to which God has called you, which you have confessed so well before many witnesses.
—*1 Timothy 6:12 NLT*

How do these verses, along with Luke 10:19, nullify the idea that you are to pray and ask God to remove the enemy from your life?

_____

_____

_____

CORE STRENGTHENER

You must know that the enemy is afraid of you. When he looks at you, he doesn't see who your friends see; he sees Christ. You are the body of Christ; you are God's anointed one. You're made in the image of the One who destroyed him and took away all his armor and weapons. You are a threat to the enemy!

2. When Satan attacked Jesus in the desert, Jesus didn't pray to the Father to stop the devil. He resisted the enemy directly. Read Matthew 4:1-11 and identify three principles Jesus demonstrated in standing against the enemy that you can apply in your own life.

Three things Jesus did that I need to do to resist the enemy are...

_____

_____

_____

_____

SETTING *the* PACE

"Spiritual warfare is the ability to discern when the devil is talking. Because when he speaks, his native language is a lie. ...You're going to have to come to a point in spiritual warfare where truth is how you fight the devil. ...The fastest way to rebuke and remove the enemy from your life is just to speak the truth."
—*Larry Stockstill*[3]

3. There is an important connection between verses 6 and 7 of James 4. Carefully read this passage and identify the vital link between *humility before God* and *the ability* (grace) *to resist the enemy.*

But he gives us more and more strength [grace] to stand against all such evil longings. As the Scripture says, God gives strength [grace] to the humble, but sets himself against the proud and haughty. So give yourselves humbly to God. **Resist the devil** *and he will flee from you.*
—James 4:6-7 TLB
[Words in brackets added for clarity.]

Why is humility required to resist the enemy? Are you clothed with it?

_____

Group leader extra: Consider Jesus' words in John 15:5 and Paul's in Romans 7:18.

FLEE

The word *flee* is the Greek word *pheugo*. It is closely related to the English word *fugitive*.[4] It means "to run away, shun, vanish, or escape."[5] The use of this word in Greek literature described a person who broke the law and fled in terror to escape being prosecuted.[6]

---

4. Have you been battling the enemy in one particular area for a long time? If so, you are not alone. Describe the fight you're in and include any patterns within the attack. In what ways have you successfully resisted the devil and seen him flee?

---

5. How has Satan tried to get you to back down from resisting him? What thoughts or feelings of discouragement, doubt, and fear has he tried to get you to accept? How is this session exposing his lies and increasing your faith to relentlessly stand against him?

The frequent thoughts and feelings Satan has brought against me include...

The way this session is encouraging and strengthening me is...

SETTING *the* PACE

"Just because the current giant you are facing looks like one you defeated in the past, don't buy the lie that you never really won the first battle! By the strength of God's grace, you trusted the Almighty and conquered your Goliath. The first giant is dead. Satan is masquerading as your former enemy so he can slip past your faith and regain entrance into your life. **Resist him.**"

—*Francis Frangipane*[7]

6. Name three areas in which Satan consistently attacks you. Using a Bible concordance or website like biblegateway.com, find Scriptures that strengthen you to resist these attacks. As you study, write down verses that jump off the page. These are *rhema* words from the Holy Spirit. Hide them in your heart, meditate on them, and speak them out loud.

Area of Attack: _____ God's Word to annihilate this attack:

_____

_____

_____

Area of Attack: _____ God's Word to annihilate this attack:

_____

_____

_____

Area of Attack: _____ God's Word to annihilate this attack:

_____

_____

_____

SETTING *the* PACE

"You'll only defeat the devil when you've got a foundation of God's Word and you act upon it. The Bible says (speaking of Satan), 'Whom resist steadfast in the faith...' (1 Peter 5:9). Your level of faith is directly related to the degree of God's Word dwelling in your heart, that is, that Word which is reality to you and in which you are daily walking."
—**Kenneth E. Hagin**[8]

STEADFAST

The word *steadfast* in 1 Peter 5:9 is the Greek word *stereos*. It means "solid, stable, strong, sure."[9] It is a synonym for *relentless*. A person who steadfastly resists the enemy is one who is unwavering, persistent, committed, loyal, dependable, constant, and immovable in their faith.

7. Persistence in our resistance pays off. That's what it means to *hold fast, be steadfast,* and *live relentlessly*. The missionary who prayed and rebuked the spirit of death from an infant sixteen times is a great example of this.

Ponder these passages on perseverance.

My dear, dear friends, stand your ground. And don't hold back. Throw yourselves into the work of the Master, confident that nothing you do for him is a waste of time or effort.

—*1 Corinthians 15:58 The Message*

Christ has set us free to live a free life. So take your stand! Never again let anyone put a harness of slavery on you.

—*Galatians 5:1 The Message*

So don't get tired of doing what is good. Don't get discouraged and give up, for we will reap a harvest of blessing at the appropriate time.

—*Galatians 6:9 NLT*

So brace up your minds; be sober (circumspect, morally alert); *set your hope wholly and unchangeably on the grace* (divine favor) *that is coming to you* when Jesus Christ (the Messiah) is revealed.

—*1 Peter 1:13 AMP*

Because you have guarded and kept My word of patient endurance [have held fast the lesson of My patience *with the expectant endurance that I give you*], I also will keep you [safe] from the hour of trial (testing) which is coming on the whole world to try those who dwell upon the earth. I am coming quickly; hold fast what you have, so that no one may rob you and deprive you of your crown.

—*Revelation 3:10-11 AMP*

What picture of perseverance develops in you as you read these verses? Where does the ability to persevere come from?

_____

_____

_____

G 8. When it comes to fighting the enemy, there are two extreme mindsets that exist among believers: one that looks for a devil behind every problem and another that chooses to ignore him, believing he will eventually just go away. What is a danger associated with each of these mindsets? How might you protect yourself from them?

The danger of looking for the devil behind every problem is...

_____

_____

_____

_____

_____

_____

CORE STRENGTHENER

The Bible doesn't teach if we resist the enemy once, he is forbidden to come back and try again. No, it's quite the opposite. He is persistent and will try again and again. This is when many Christians get discouraged and experience defeat. They think, *I guess it doesn't work* or *I must not have what it takes.* These are huge lies. We cannot afford to entertain these thoughts—ever.

The danger of ignoring the enemy and believing he will just go away is...

_____

_____

_____

SOBER and VIGILANT

Sober is from the Greek word *nepho,*[10] meaning "to be free from the influence of intoxicants."[11] Thayer says sober is "to be calm and collected in spirit, self-controlled, cautious."[12] Essentially, being sober means we're clear-headed, not drawing our satisfaction from or having an inordinate attachment to anything in the world over and above God. Jesus is our first love and passion.

Vigilant is derived from the Greek word *gregoreo.* It means "to be on guard, to be watchful, or to be attentive *continually,*" and it signifies one who is on the lookout to make sure no enemy can successfully gain entrance into his home or life.[13]

---

9. Although Satan has been defeated, he is still a worthy opponent. Therefore, God charges us to be *sober* at all times. This does not just refer to the consumption of alcohol. It also pertains to the drunkenness caused by overindulgence in the pleasures of this world. Pause and take an honest look at your life. Are you *intoxicated* with anything of this world? If so, what is it and what is God prompting you to do to change it?

    Consider *work or business, a sport, a hobby, food, the Internet, television, movies, music, members of the opposite sex, shopping, etc.*

    I am intoxicated with:

    _____

    _____

    The action God is asking me to take toward proper balance is:

    _____

    _____

Don't live carelessly, unthinkingly. Make sure you understand what the Master wants. Don't drink too much wine [which includes the world's pleasures]. That cheapens your life. Drink the Spirit of God, huge draughts of him.
—Ephesians 5:17-18 The Message
[Words in brackets added for clarity.]

G 10. Being *vigilant* is not an every-now-and-then activity. It's a state of spiritual alertness we cultivate and continue in. Being vigilant protects us, especially when we're tested and tempted. Jesus told His disciples to watch—be *vigilant*—and pray with Him the night He was arrested. Carefully consider what He told them when He found them asleep:

> All of you must keep awake (give strict attention, be cautious and active) and watch and pray, that you may not come into temptation. The spirit indeed is willing, but the flesh is weak.
>
> —*Matthew 26:41 AMP*

> Keep awake and watch and pray [constantly], that you may not enter into temptation; the spirit indeed is willing, but the flesh is weak.
>
> —*Mark 14:38 AMP*

What connection is the Holy Spirit showing you between being vigilantly sober and experiencing victory?

_____

_____

_____

_____

Group leader extra: The account of Jesus in Gethsemane is found in Matthew 26:36-56, Mark 14:32-53, Luke 22:39-53, John 18:1-12.

CORE STRENGTHENER

You're sons of Light, daughters of Day. We live under wide open skies and know where we stand. So let's not sleepwalk through life like those others. Let's keep our eyes open and be smart. People sleep at night and get drunk at night. But not us! Since we're creatures of Day, let's act like it. Walk out into the daylight sober, dressed up in faith, love and the hope of salvation.
—1 Thessalonians 5:5-8 The Message

What you do not confront will not change. Your determination to be free from bondage must be greater than the adversary's determination to enslave and destroy you. Be relentless in resisting the devil. Rebuke him directly and sternly in the authority vested in you by the Lord Jesus Christ.

Are you tired of the enemy harassing you? Are you ready to take a stand against him? Are you ready to relentlessly resist him until he flees? Find a secluded place in your home or outdoors and begin to fight the enemy. Use the sword of the Spirit and speak the Word vehemently against Satan. Flip back through this study guide and find the scriptures God has brought to life during your study. Personalize them and speak them out loud against the enemy.

Prayer to Relentlessly Resist the Enemy

Father, Thank You for this session on resisting the enemy. I don't want to be silent against him anymore. Help me, God. Light Your fire in me—a fire that is fueled by Your Word and Spirit. Give me Your faith—faith to see beyond the circumstances. When the enemy attacks me or those in my sphere of influence, may Your holy anger rise up within me and speak violently against him. I no longer want to just think about scriptures. I want to speak them boldly. Forgive me for ever being angry at You or others. Help me aim my anger in the right direction. Let my words be Your words. Destroy the works of the devil through me. By your grace I am relentless. Thank You, Father. In Jesus' name, Amen.

Weekly

Read again your list of attacks and Scriptures from question 6. These attacks may be things you face daily, or they may be assaults you have ignored out of ignorance or in hopes that the devil would tire and disappear. Dedicate yourself to standing against the devil in these areas this week. Remember that your eyes are to be fixed on Jesus: you are not hunting for demonic activity but rather addressing something that clearly stands between you and God's best for you. Meditate on Scriptures that reveal your authority and the promises of God in the situation. With conviction, verbally resist the devil and claim the truth of God's Word over your life.

Day 1 **WAKE UP!**

Awake, O sleeper, and arise from the dead, and Christ shall shine (make day dawn) upon you and give you light. Look carefully then how you walk! Live purposefully and worthily and accurately, not as the unwise and witless, but as wise (sensible, intelligent people), making the very most of the time [buying up each opportunity], because the days are evil. Therefore do not be vague and thoughtless and foolish, but understanding and firmly grasping what the will of the Lord is. And do not get drunk with wine...but ever be filled and stimulated with the [Holy] Spirit.

—Ephesians 5:14-18 AMP

Can you hear it? It's just like the sound you hear every morning telling you to wake up and get moving. Right now God is sounding an alarm in the spirit, telling us to wake up, get dressed, and get to work. God doesn't want His body asleep. He wants us awake, sober, and vigilant, ruling in life and advancing His Kingdom.

When your alarm goes off each morning, you get up, get dressed, and go to work. How does this compare to your spiritual life? *Consider* Romans 13:11-14, Ephesians 6:10-18, and John 9:4.

In regard to Christ's return, what are the dangers of being asleep? What are the rewards of being awake? *Read* Matthew 24:36-51; Revelation 3:2-3, 16:15 and 1 Thessalonians 4:13-18, 5:1-11.

The dangers of being asleep are...

The rewards of being awake are...

Related scriptures: Luke 12:35-40

Child of the Most High, the Spirit of God is sounding the alarm to resurrect His Body. Don't let a moment go to waste. Warnings have been given. The end is in sight. Don't hit the snooze button. Wake up, get dressed, and get to work!

Day 2 UNDERSTAND HOW THE DEVIL OPERATES

After all, we don't want to unwittingly give Satan an opening for yet more mischief—we're not oblivious to his sly ways!

—2 Corinthians 2:11 The Message

There are some interesting truths in the meaning of the word *devil*. To understand its meaning is to understand Satan's primary mode of operation. Author, pastor, and Greek scholar **Rick Renner** offers this powerful insight:

"The word 'devil' is a compound of the words *dia* and *balos*. The word *dia*...means *through*, as *to pierce something from one side all the way through to the other side*. The word *balos* means *to throw*, as when a person throws a ball, a rock, or some other object. When these two words are joined, it means *to repetitiously throw something—striking again and again and again until the object being struck has finally been completely penetrated.*

...[The enemy] comes to assault the **mind**—not once but many times. ...As soon as the victim lets down his mental resistance, the devil gives one last firm punch that finally succeeds in penetrating his mind."[14]

SETTING *the* PACE

"Every Christian must deal with a two-fold problem in his mind. First, he must root out and destroy the practiced tracks of thinking he may never have realized are bondages. Without help he cannot do this. Secondly, he must seek new rootage in the Spirit, in the mind of Christ. ...The mind of Christ in us is a fountain of eternal wisdom and freedom of thought. But we must let go the old tracks of thought and learn to sink our roots into Jesus and build ways of letting His mind fill all the channels of our thinking processes."

—*John L. and R. Loren Sandford*[15]

As soon as the enemy has penetrated a person's mind, he floods it with lies, doubt, fear, worry, anger, strife, and even false interpretation of Scripture. Why? He wants control of our minds because the content of our minds fills the corridors of our hearts and directs the course of our lives.

What new understanding is the Holy Spirit giving you through the meaning of the devil's name?

Can you remember a time you resisted the enemy and he fled? Describe what happened.

Knowing Satan's primary mode of operation is to repeatedly strike you with things like doubt, deception, and fear, why is it important for you to renew your mind with God's Word?

Day 3 AIM YOUR ANGER IN THE RIGHT DIRECTION

"Be angry, and do not sin": do not let the sun go down on your wrath, nor give place to the devil.

—Ephesians 4:26-27 NKJV

Being angry is not necessarily a sin. It is what we do with our anger that can get us in trouble. As we learned earlier, we are in a spiritual war, and we are *not* fighting against people. We are battling the devil and his demonic forces. Maintaining this sobering viewpoint is vital and protects us from fighting with people, thus being blindsided by the enemy.

Righteous anger is appropriate and can motivate us to advance God's Kingdom. God Himself has displayed righteous anger many times. Jesus was angry, yet He did *not* sin. At both the beginning and end of His ministry, He visibly displayed anger when He cleared the temple (see Matthew 21:12-13, Mark 11:15-19, Luke 19:41-46, John 2:13-17). If we are angry at the things that anger God and handle ourselves the way He does, anger can be a positive thing.

According to Scripture, what makes God angry? *Read* Numbers 11:1-10, 12:1-9, 25:1-3; Joshua 7:1; Judges 2:11-14; Proverbs 6:16-19; Hebrews 10:26-27.

Clearly, God does not want us to harbor or direct anger toward people. Read Ephesians 4:26-27. How and when are you to deal with anger toward others? Why is this so vital, and what will happen if you don't deal with anger appropriately?

What quickly and consistently makes you angry? How about when trials hit?

Do you tend to get angry at God when troubles come? If so, why? Ask Him to show the root reasons in your heart. Write what He reveals and surrender it to Him.

How can you better direct your anger toward the enemy, the source of all tribulation?

Day 4 RELEASE THE POWER RIGHT UNDER YOUR NOSE

The tongue has the power of life and death, and those who love it will eat its fruit.
—Proverbs 18:21 NIV

How many times have you looked and looked for something only to find it was right under your nose? Something similar takes place in our fight against the enemy. The answers to our problems are found in fellowship with the Father—in the power of His Word and the presence of His Spirit. Releasing this power into reality is done through speaking. Minister and author **Charles Capps** says,

"The body of Christ must begin to live in the authority of the Word. For God's Word is creative power. That Creative power is produced by the heart, formed by the tongue, and released out of the mouth in word form."[16]

Satan wants us to agree with and confess his words of doubt, fear, and death. God wants us to agree with and confess His words of faith, power, and life found in Scripture and spoken to us by His Spirit. When spoken aloud, the explosive rhema words He drops in our heart are like atomic bombs against the enemy.

When the enemy attacks, what is your response? What comes out of your mouth?

_____

_____

Ask God to help you guard your mouth: Psalm 141:3; Proverbs 13, 21:23; Philippians 2:14; 1 Peter 3:10-12.

To effectively resist the enemy, you have to speak the Word to him. Are you? If not, why? Ask the Lord to show you what hinders you and what will change it.

_____

_____

No word from God shall be without power or impossible of fulfillment.
—Luke 1:37 AMP

Slowly read Romans 4:17, Ephesians 5:1, and Jeremiah 23:28-29. Note our heavenly Father's character, His words, and our response. What do these verses reveal about speaking God's Word?

_____

_____

When you're being attacked, don't just *read* the Word—**speak** it. Don't just *think* about Scriptures—**speak** them. Turn the everlasting Word of God into the indestructible weapon He meant it to be! Use it to resist the enemy and he will flee!

Day 5 JESUS IS THE REAL DEAL

"Look! The Lion of the tribe of Judah, the Root of David, has conquered, and proved himself worthy to open the scroll and to break its seven seals."
—Revelation 5:5 TLB

The devil is *not* a lion. Jesus is—the Lion of the tribe of Judah. And there is no similarity between Jesus and Satan. Jesus is the real deal!

Remember, Satan and his fallen angels have been disarmed. Colossians 2:15 declares that God "stripped all the spiritual tyrants in the universe of their sham authority at the Cross and marched them naked through the streets" (The Message). God has defeated the enemy!

Although Satan has been disarmed, he and his cohorts are still formidable foes. How can you enforce the victory Christ won at Calvary? To answer this, let's look at three principles for protecting yourself from a roaming lion in the wild:

1. **Keep your campfire burning**. Lions are afraid of fire.[17]

2. **Stay together with your group. Don't separate from each other.** Lions are known to attack and kill a straggler who is doing his own thing.[18]

3. **If you encounter a lion, stand still and flat-footed. Do not run.** Look the lion straight in the eyes, raise your arms, and make the loudest noises you can. If you run, the lion will pounce on you and eat you alive.[19]

Apply these principles to your Christian walk and your resistance to the enemy.

What do you think it means to *keep your campfire burning*, and how does it protect you? Consider Matthew 3:11; Luke 12:49, 24:27-32; Acts 2:1-4, 4:8-13 and Jeremiah 20:9.

_____

_____

How does *staying with your group* apply to you as a part of Christ? Consider Hebrews 10:25, Ecclesiastes 4:9-12, Acts 4:31-35, and 1 Corinthians 12:12-27.

_____

_____

What protection is found by *standing still and not running* from the enemy? Consider Ephesians 6:13, 1 Corinthians 15:58, Galatians 5:1, and 1 Peter 5:8-9.

_____

_____

Day 6 MAKE CHRIST YOUR FIRST LOVE

"Turn back! Recover your dear early love. No time to waste."
—Revelation 2:5 The Message

Do you remember when you first accepted Christ as your Lord and Savior? Those early days were sweet. Fresh revelation of all He has done for you caused your eyes to swell with grateful tears. But since then, the difficulties of life and the passage of time may have caused the luster of your love to tarnish. It's not the same as it used to be.

If the enemy is getting the best of you and your levels of faith and power have diminished, you may have lost your first love. Your affection for the Lord may have taken a backseat to something or someone else, like entertainment, recreation, or a new friend. Keep in mind that what you eat is what you will hunger for. The enemy does not care how long it takes or what he has to do to break your fellowship with the Lord as long as he accomplishes his task.

Take an honest look at your relationship with Christ. How would you describe it: on-fire, a medium flame, or barely a flicker? Ask God to show you why.

_____

_____

Reigniting your passion for Christ and His Word starts with repentance. After Jesus told the church at Ephesus they had lost their first love, He told them to "repent and do the things [they] did at first" (Revelation 2:5 NIV). What things formerly fanned your fire of desire for God? What must change to do them again?

_____

_____

The power to stand steadfastly against the enemy is inseparably linked to abiding in Christ. Carefully read Jesus' words in John 15:1-17. What new insight is the Holy Spirit revealing about having a vibrant relationship with the Lord?

_____

_____

_____

SETTING *the* PACE

"It isn't necessary that we stay in church in order to remain in God's presence. We can make our hearts personal chapels where we can enter anytime to talk to God privately. These conversations can be so loving and gentle, and anyone can have them. Is there any reason not to begin? He may be waiting for us to take the first step. ...Gradually train yourself to show your love for Him by asking for His grace. Offer your heart to Him at every moment. Don't restrict your love of Him with rules or special devotions. Go out in faith, with love and humility."
—*Brother Lawrence*[20]

SESSION SUMMARY

We are in a spiritual war, and God wants us alert and watchful of what is going on. When the enemy strikes, He wants *us* to take the weapons He has provided and resist the devil steadfastly until he flees. We are to open our mouths and declare God's Word directly and fiercely against Satan and his fallen foes until the attack is broken.

Notes

_____

(1) Adapted from *Strong's Exhaustive Concordance of the Bible*, James Strong, LL.D., S.T.D. (Nashville, TN: Thomas Nelson Publishers, 1990). (2) Adapted from *Sparkling Gems from the Greek*, Rick Renner (Tulsa, OK: Teach All Nations, 2003) p. 942. (3) *Delivered from the Lion*, audio series by Larry Stockstill, *Part 2 - The Truth* (Baton Rouge, LA: Bethany World Prayer Center). (4) Adapted from *Vine's Complete Expository Dictionary of Old and New Testament Words*, W.E. Vine (Nashville, TN: Thomas Nelson Publishing, 1996) p. 242. (5) See note 1. (6) See note 2, p. 943. (7) Christian quotes on *Spiritual Warfare* (retrieved 8/5/11 from http://dailychristianquote.com/dcqspiritwarfare2.html). (8) Kenneth E. Hagin, *The Believer's Authority* (Tulsa, OK: Rhema Bible Church, 2007) p. 62. (9) See note 1. (10) Ibid. (11) See note 4, p. 583. (12) Adapted from *Thayer's Greek-English Lexicon of the New Testament*, Joseph H. Thayer (Grand Rapids, MI: Baker Book House Company, 1977) p. 425. (13) See note 2, p. 652. (14) Ibid., p. 942. (15) John L. Sandford and R. Loren Sandford, *The Renewal of the Mind* (Tulsa, OK: Victory House Publishers, 1991) pp. 19-20. (16) Charles Capps, *God's Creative Power* (Tulsa, OK: Harrison House, 1976) p. 8. (17) *Delivered from the Lion*, audio series by Larry Stockstill, *Part 1 – Satan's Weapons* (Baton Rouge, LA: Bethany World Prayer Center). (18) Ibid. (19) Adapted from *Time's Up Devil*, audio message by Perry Stone (Cleveland, TN: Voice of Evangelism, www.perrystone.org). (20) Brother Lawrence, *The Practice of the Presence of God* (New Kensington, PA: Whitaker House, 1982) pp. 37-38.

> *Submit* yourselves, then,
> to God. Resist the devil,
> and he will flee from you.
>
> **—James 4:7 NIV**

THE HIGHEST FORM OF RESISTANCE

Please refer to session 10 of the teaching series, along with chapter 14 in the Relentless book.

G 1. Submitting to God means *obeying* Him. It means doing what He says regardless of whether we like it or understand it. In what ways has your life been blessed in the past because of *your* obedience?

_____

_____

_____

_____

_____

_____

_____

_____

_____

_____

_____

CORE STRENGTHENER

The foremost method of resisting the devil is to **submit to God**. This means living in consistent trust and obedience to Him. By doing so, we can usher His ways, His mindset, and His principles into the twisted and perverted areas of the world around us. *Absolute obedience* is the principal method of fighting off the strongholds and attacks of the enemy and the way we can rise to a new level of authority and rulership.

OBEDIENCE

To *obey* means "to comply with the commands or instructions of a superior or with the requirements of law—moral or political; to submit to the government, direction or control of another." To obey also means "to not do that which is prohibited." When we're obedient to God or the authority He's established, we "submit to Him, performing what is required and abstaining from what is forbidden."[1] It is vital to realize that **the power to relentlessly obey is found in God's grace**.

G 2. Obeying God includes obeying the people He has placed over us at home, at work, and in ministry. In what situation should we *not* obey those in authority over us? Consider Jesus' instructions and the apostles' words in these verses:

> [Jesus] said to them, "Go into all the world and preach the good news to all creation."
>
> —*Mark 16:15 NIV*

> Go then and make disciples of all the nations, baptizing them into the name of the Father and of the Son and of the Holy Spirit, teaching them to observe everything that I have commanded you.
>
> —*Matthew 28:19-20 AMP*

> So they called the apostles back in and told them never again to speak or teach about Jesus. But Peter and John replied, "Do you think God wants us to obey you rather than him? We cannot stop telling about the wonderful things we have seen and heard."
>
> —*Acts 4:18-20 NLT*

_____

_____

_____

SETTING *the* PACE

"God is God. Because He is God, *He is worthy of my trust and obedience.* I will find rest nowhere but in His holy will, a will that is unspeakably beyond my largest notions of what He is up to."
—*Elisabeth Elliot*[2]

CORE STRENGTHENER

Spiritual growth doesn't come when the sun shines brightly on our lives, when everyone speaks well of us and treats us nicely, and everything goes smoothly. No, we grow spiritually when all hell is breaking loose in our lives and *we choose to still obey God* in the midst of it.

3. Is there something God has asked you to do that you have not done? Is there something He's asked you *not* to do that you are doing? Humble yourself before Him and ask Him to show you any instruction you have not obeyed. Write what He reveals, and ask Him for grace to take action and carry it out.

_____

_____

_____

_____

_____

4. When we are born into the Kingdom of God, we
G are not born as spiritual adults but as babies. We then grow up spiritually in God's grace as we abide in Christ. While physical growth is a result of *time* and intellectual growth is a result of *learning*, **spiritual growth** is a result or function of *suffering* and *obedience*.

1 PETER 4:1-2

So, since Christ suffered in the flesh for us, for you, arm yourselves with the same thought and purpose [patiently to suffer rather than fail to please God]. For whoever has suffered in the flesh [having the mind of Christ] is done with [intentional] sin [has stopped pleasing himself and the world, and pleases God], so that he can no longer spend the rest of his natural life living by [his] human appetites and desires, but [he lives] for what God wills.

—AMP

Since Jesus went through everything you're going through and more, learn to think like him. Think of your sufferings as a weaning from that old sinful habit of always expecting to get your own way. Then you'll be able to live out your days free to pursue what God wants instead of being tyrannized by what you want.

—The Message

HEBREWS 5:8

Even though Jesus was God's Son, he learned obedience from the things he suffered.

—NLT

Jesus is God's own Son, but still he had to suffer before he could learn what it really means to obey God.

—CEV

How do these scriptures explain and help clarify the principle of growing up spiritually?

_____

_____

_____

When I was a child, I spoke as a child, I understood as a child, I thought
as a child; but when I became a man, I put away childish things.
—1 Corinthians 13:11 NKJV

G 5. Carefully read 1 Corinthians 2:15-16, 3:1-3; Ephesians 4:13-15; Hebrews 5:12-14; 2 Thessalonians 1:3-4 and James 3:2. What are the characteristics of the *carnal, immature* Christian and the *spiritual, mature* believer? Which do you find yourself identifying with more, and what evidence in your life confirms this?

The carnal, immature Christian:

_____

_____

_____

The spiritual, mature believer:

_____

_____

_____

Group leader extra: Consider Jesus' words to Peter in John 21:18.

I identify more with _____. The evidence confirming this:

_____

_____

_____

Character Profile
JOSEPH
_____

Lifespan: 110 years—1915 B.C to 1805 B.C.3
Occupation: Shepherd, slave, prison overseer, second-in-command over all of Egypt
Place of Service: Lands of Canaan and Egypt
Relatives: Parents: Jacob and Rachel; Grandfather: Isaac; eleven brothers (see names below), one sister (Dinah); Wife: Asenath; Sons: Ephraim and Manasseh.
Words Describing Joseph: Loyal, uncompromising, forgiving, merciful, discerning, wise, relentless

Joseph's name means "May God add." It was later changed by Pharaoh to *Zaph-nath-Paaneah*, meaning "revealer of secrets."[4] He was the eleventh-born son of Jacob and had eleven brothers, each a head of a tribe of Israel. They were, in birth order: Reuben, Simeon, Levi, Judah, Dan, Naphtali, Gad, Asher, Issachar, Zebulun, and Benjamin. Joseph was highly favored by his father—mainly because he was the firstborn of Jacob's favorite wife, Rachel. Joseph was so adored by his father that his sons, Ephraim and Manasseh, were adopted by Jacob, allowing Joseph's lineage to have a double share in Israel's inheritance (see Genesis 48:1-6).

Joseph's relentless faith and obedience in the midst of hardships positioned him to be one of the most powerful rulers on the face of the earth during a time of widespread famine. He made a way for his father, Jacob, and all the tribes of Israel not only to be kept safe but also to multiply abundantly. The provision and protection in Egypt, though it eventually became their prophesied bondage (see Genesis 15:13), set up the next major phase of Israel's history: the exodus.

Joseph ruled in Egypt for nearly **80 years** (see Genesis 41:46, 50:26). Read his full story in Genesis 30-50. What can you learn from his life and apply in your own?

---

6. Joseph was highly favored by his father and given a dream by God that he would rule in life. As a result, his brothers despised him and sold him into slavery. He spent many years serving Potiphar and was then thrown into

prison for a crime he didn't commit. In what ways can you personally identify with Joseph's unfair treatment?

_____

_____

_____

7. While serving Potiphar, Joseph chose to obey God and refused the advances of his master's wife. As a result, he was thrown in a dungeon. Have you experienced a situation in which you obeyed God and were punished? Has the enemy attacked you with thoughts that accused God or insulted His character? Are you second-guessing your decision to serve God? Carefully meditate on these truths from God's Word.

> I know the plans that I have for you, declares the Lord. They are plans for peace and not disaster, plans to give you a future filled with hope.
> —*Jeremiah 29:11 GW*

> How precious are your thoughts about me, O God. They cannot be numbered! I can't even count them; they outnumber the grains of sand! And when I wake up, you are still with me!
> —*Psalm 139:17-18 NLT*

> **SETTING** *the* **PACE**
>
> "In any trial, in any bitter situation, you are not alone, you are not helpless, you are not a victim. You have a tree, a cross, shown to you by the Sovereign God of Calvary. Whatever the trial or temptation, it is not more than you can bear. It is bearable. It can be handled. You can know as Joseph knew, 'You meant evil against me, but God meant it for good in order to bring about this present result, to preserve many people alive' (Genesis 50:20)."
> —*Kay Arthur*[5]

> Everything God does is right—the trademark on all his works is love. God's there, listening for all who pray, for all who pray and mean it. He does what's best for those who fear him—hears them call out, and saves them. God sticks by all who love him.
> —*Psalm 145:17-20 The Message*

> "My thoughts are nothing like your thoughts," says the Lord. "And my ways are far beyond anything you could imagine. For just as the heavens are higher than the earth, so my ways are higher than your ways and my thoughts higher than your thoughts.
> —*Isaiah 55:8-9 NLT*

> Oh, what a wonderful God we have! How great are his wisdom and knowledge and riches! How impossible it is for us to understand his decisions and his methods!
> —*Romans 11:33 TLB*

How do these scriptures help you see your situation in a different, more hopeful light?

_____

_____

Think About it...

Dr. Victor E. Frankl, survivor of three grim years at Auschwitz and other Nazi prisons, recorded this observation on life in Hitler's camps:

"We who lived in concentration camps can remember the men who walked through the huts comforting others, giving away their last piece of bread. They have been few in number, but they offer sufficient proof that *everything can be taken from man but one thing: the last of the human freedoms—to choose one's attitude in any given set of circumstances.*"[6]

---

8. When Joseph first received his God-given dream of ruling in life, he had *immature, fleshly* qualities in his character that needed to die in order for God's plan to thrive. Are you in the midst of a trial and feel like you're dying inside? If so, what aspects of your character is God trying to put to death so that His plan may come to life? How can you better cooperate with Him?

The immature aspects of my character that need to die are...

_____

_____

I believe I can better cooperate with God by...

_____

_____

_____

Think About It...

If Joseph would have taken revenge and killed his brothers, look who would not have been born:

Levi's notable descendants: Aaron, Moses, Ezra, and John the Baptist
Benjamin's notable descendants: Saul, Esther, and the apostle Paul
Judah's notable descendants: Caleb, David, Solomon, and Jesus Christ

What would life have been like without these people?

> ## CHARACTER
> Most of us understand that *character* is "the unique qualities of a person that distinguish him from others—most often they are good qualities that are esteemed and respected." Interestingly, the literal meaning of the word character is taken from a Greek word meaning "to scrape, cut or engrave."[7] For us to have the character of Christ means He has marked or impressed in us His person. By being in His presence and going through life's difficulties, His image has been *scraped*, *cut*, and *engraved* into who we are.

9. Look back at the trials God has brought you through. What immature or ungodly qualities has He removed from your character as a result of your obedience through suffering? What mind-sets and behaviors, that were once strongholds, are no longer active in your life? How does recalling what He's done strengthen you to press on?

Past Trial	Immature, Ungodly Mind-sets and Behaviors God Removed	How God Shaped Me and Made Me More Like Christ

Recalling what God has done strengthens me to press on because...

_____

_____

_____

_____

_____

_____

_____

_____

_____

_____

CORE STRENGTHENER

We must see adversity through the right perspective. It's not God-given, but rather God-permitted, and it is beneficial if handled correctly. It's designed as the vehicle to carry you to your place of rulership. Your obedience to God's Word in the midst of hardship will *perfect, establish, strengthen,* and *settle* you to fulfill your destiny.

10. Are you ready to grow beyond your present situation? Then instead of asking God "Why?" when things go wrong, begin asking Him, "What should I do, Lord?" Instead of seeing each tribulation as a *setback*, how can you understand it as a *step forward*? Pray and ask the Lord for His insight. Write what He speaks to you.

_____

_____

_____

_____

SETTING *the* PACE

"**'All the paths of the Lord are loving and faithful'**
(Psalm 25:10). I have pondered this verse lately, and have found that it feeds my spirit. All does not mean 'all, except the paths I am walking in now' or 'nearly all, except this especially difficult and painful path.' All must mean all. So, your path with its unexplained sorrow or turmoil, and mine with its sharp flints and briers—and both our paths, with their unexplained perplexity, their sheer mystery—they are His paths, on which He will show Himself loving and faithful. Nothing else; nothing less."
—Amy Carmichael[8]

Weekly CHALLENGE

Identify an important relationship that you have given up on, maybe one with a family member. Perhaps you have allowed offenses or arguments to sabotage your relationship. Be relentless in your efforts toward reconciliation. In prayer, ask for the grace to put aside past frustration or hurt. Identify the heart of God for restoration and intentionally reach out to this person with love.

Day 1 WHAT ARE STRONGHOLDS?

We do not war according to the flesh. For the weapons of our warfare are not carnal but mighty in God for pulling down **strongholds***.*

—2 Corinthians 10:3-4 NKJV

We are in a spiritual war, and only the spiritual weapons provided and empowered by God's grace will destroy the works of the enemy, including the strongholds in our lives. What are strongholds?

> ### STRONGHOLD
> The word *stronghold* is derived from the Greek verb *ochuroma*, meaning "to fortify with the idea of holding something safely." It's the same word used for "a castle or fortress."[9] In 2 Corinthians 10:4, strongholds signify "a castle or fortress of thoughts—arguments and reasonings the enemy develops and fortifies in our minds.[10] Interestingly, *ochuroma* was a word used during New Testament times to also describe a *prison.* Therefore, strongholds act as both a castle and a prison of thoughts—they prevent truth from getting in and keep lies from getting out. Strongholds are patterns of thinking that are so ingrained in our mind they influence and control certain areas of our lives.[11]

Carefully reread the definition of a stronghold. What areas in your life fit this description? Where do you have a *natural inclination* to believe, speak, and act in agreement with the enemy?

_____

It what ways have these strongholds functioned as a *fortress*? Have they kept you separated from certain people or opportunities?

_____

How have these strongholds acted like a *prison*? How have they held you back from fulfilling your destiny and ruling in life?

_____

The tribulations (*thlipsis*) the Lord permits to come our way put just enough pressure in just the right places to reveal ungodly strongholds in our thinking. When the pressure is on, what's inside of us comes out. When all hell breaks loose in our lives, our thoughts, actions, and words reveal where our character is out of sync with God's nature. Through the difficulty, God is shaping us to be more like Christ. He is revealing something in our character that has to change in order for us to enter a higher level of His supreme, powerful rule. This is the positive outcome of adversity.

Day 2 HOW ARE STRONGHOLDS BUILT?

Neither give place to the devil.

—Ephesians 4:27 KJV

How are strongholds built? By *giving place* to the enemy. The Greek word for *place* literally means "a space, position or occupancy."[12] Figuratively, it indicates "opportunity, power, or occasion for acting."[13] So when God says *don't give place to the enemy*, He's telling us "don't give Satan an opportunity to produce his character in your life. Don't rent him any space."

Every time the enemy brings us a negative, ungodly thought, he is trying to gain space in our thinking. A doubt here, a worry there, an accusation about this person, a thought of jealousy about that person... First he gains a toehold, then a foothold, until finally he has a stronghold. If we *accept* his lies, we give him place. He will erect his castle in our minds and begin dominating areas of our lives.

CORE STRENGTHENER

The real threat is not our adverse circumstances, but *wrong beliefs* and *thoughts* that try to slip in during our hardship. We must be relentless in our belief and firm to resist any logic or thinking contrary to God's Word.

Now think: What thoughts is Satan repeatedly bringing against your mind and emotions?

The stronghold is _____. The thoughts Satan brings include...

_____

_____

The stronghold is _____. The thoughts Satan brings include...

_____

The stronghold is _____. The thoughts Satan brings include...

_____

Examine what's going on when these thoughts come. What circumstances are you facing? What are you reading, watching, or listening to? Who are you hanging around? Ask God for discernment and a plan to guard yourself in the future.

_____

_____

Realize that not rejecting thoughts from the enemy means you accept them by default. There is no neutral ground. Satan is out to kill, steal, and destroy. But you don't have to listen to him. By God's grace, you have been given His armor to effectively defeat the enemy! As you recognize and resist him, you will win the fight!

Day 3 HOW ARE STRONGHOLDS DESTROYED?

For the weapons of our warfare are not carnal but mighty in God for pulling down strongholds, casting down arguments and every high thing that exalts itself against the knowledge of God, bringing every thought into captivity to the obedience of Christ.

—2 Corinthians 10:4-5 NKJV

Once you identify a stronghold, destroy it with the weapons of grace. Suppose you recognize a stronghold of *fear* in your life. First, repent of giving place to the enemy through fear. Repentance is a complete change of mind, an acceptance of what God says over our own experiences or beliefs. When we repent, we experience the renewal of our minds by what God has spoken (Romans 12:2).

Next, you must **speak** destruction against the stronghold of fear. This is how you *release the power right under your nose*, the power of life and death in your words (Proverbs 18:21). You can say, "In the name of Jesus, I have not been given a spirit of fear (2 Timothy 1:7). You spirit of fear, get out of my life! You have no authority over me. God has given me *all* authority over you (Luke 10:19), and I'm enforcing it now." This type of resistance can be used against any stronghold you are facing, from fear and worry to anger and strife.

2 Corinthians says we are to "cast down **arguments** and every **high thing** that exalts itself." The King James Version includes **imaginations**. What mindsets in your life are trying to rise above and replace God's Word?

_____

_____

_____

Remember, strongholds are castles or prisons of thinking that are fortified— *made stronger*—by the enemy's lies. Pray and ask God to show you any influences, activities, or relationships that are fortifying strongholds in you. You need to *throw off* these weights. Write what He reveals.

_____

_____

What scriptures directly counter the strongholds you're dealing with? Write them out, hide them in your heart, and speak them against the enemy.

_____

_____

_____

If you don't know any scriptures that counter the enemy's lies in these areas, dig into God's Word and find some. Use a Bible concordance or search for keywords online.

Day 4 BUILD STRONGHOLDS OF RIGHTEOUSNESS

Build me up again by your Word. Barricade the road that goes Nowhere; grace me with your clear revelation.

—Psalm 119:28-29 The Message

Once you've identified a stronghold and spoken its destruction, there is one more crucial step. You must **fill the space** the enemy once occupied. Jesus explains in Matthew 12:43-45: "When an evil spirit leaves a person, it goes into the desert, seeking rest but finding none. Then it says, 'I will return to the person I came from.' So it returns and finds its former home *empty*, swept, and in order. Then the spirit finds seven other spirits more evil than itself, and they all enter the person and live there. And so that person is worse off than before" (NLT).

In order to prevent this, we must pray and ask God to build a stronghold of righteousness in the place the enemy once occupied. We must feed ourselves a steady diet of God's presence and His Word, especially scriptures that counter the perverted thinking that once held us hostage. Each verse we take in becomes a building block for the Holy Spirit.

Carefully read Philippians 1:9-11; Matthew 4:4; John 6:35, 48-51; Colossians 3:16; 1 Peter 2:2 and Jeremiah 15:16. What do these verses say to you about building strongholds of righteousness?

_____

_____

According to Jesus' words in Matthew 7:24-27, what else is vital to successful building?

_____

Related scripture: James 1:22-25

> *"Break new ground. **Plant righteousness**, and harvest the fruit that your loyalty will produce for me." It's time to seek the Lord! When he comes, he will rain righteousness on you.*
> —Hosea 10:12 GW

Are you consuming anything that spoils your appetite for God?

_____

What are some practical ways to increase your spiritual appetite for God's presence and Word?

_____

_____

Day 5 THE STRONGHOLD OF OBEDIENCE IS REWARDING

If you are willing and obedient, you will eat the best from the land.

—Isaiah 1:19 NIV

Obedience to God is the highest form of resistance against the enemy.

Read 1 John 3:24, Matthew 12:50, Exodus 19:5, Deuteronomy 11:8-9, and 1 Kings 3:14. Name the blessings of obeying God shared in these verses.

Related passage: Deuteronomy 28:1-14

According to John 14:23, 1 John 5:3, and 2 John 1:6, what does your obedience demonstrate?

If we obey God in the midst of suffering, we will be blessed. Meditate on the message of these promises. How do they motivate you to obey the Lord?

Can anyone really harm you for being eager to do good deeds? Even if you have to suffer for doing good things, God will bless you. So stop being afraid and don't worry about what people might do.

—1 Peter 3:13-14 CEV

Friends, when life gets really difficult, don't jump to the conclusion that God isn't on the job. Instead, be glad that you are in the very thick of what Christ experienced. This is a spiritual refining process, with glory just around the corner. So be happy when you are insulted for being a Christian, for then the glorious Spirit of God rests upon you.

—1 Peter 4:12-14 The Message & NLT

In his kindness God called you to share in his eternal glory by means of Christ Jesus. So after you have suffered a little while, he will restore, support, and strengthen you, and he will place you on a firm foundation.

—1 Peter 5:10 NLT

In what area(s) of your life do you find it hardest to obey God? Pray and ask the Lord to show you why this is the case. Ask Him for His perspective and how He wants you to respond. Write what He reveals.

Day 6 DON'T ABORT YOUR DREAM

*Hope deferred makes the heart sick, but a **dream** fulfilled is a tree of life.*
—Proverbs 13:12 NLT

Are you pregnant with a dream from God? Just like a woman becomes pregnant through her intimate relationship with her husband, we become pregnant with divine dreams through intimacy with Christ. He loves you and desires to birth new things in and through your life. Relentless faith in God's promises is the pathway to your destiny. *Believing* what He said to you in His Word and by His Spirit, even in the midst of adversity, will bring those dreams to pass.

CORE STRENGTHENER

When all hell is breaking loose, when it seems like nothing is going right, *stand*! It doesn't matter how many weeks or months have passed, *stand*. After you have done all you know to do, *stand*. **Stand on the truth** because truth endures the test of time! No man, woman, or devil can ever get you out of God's will! No one but God holds your destiny.

Has God given you a dream that your family or friends do not understand? Briefly describe it, including any confirmations He has given you.

The dream God has given me and how He has confirmed it:

_____

_____

Carefully read Hebrews 10:35-39 and James 1:3-4. Why has your dream been delayed? What is God developing in you?

_____

_____

Only one person can destroy your destiny: *you*. The greatest threat to your dream is *unbelief*. Unbelief caused the people of Israel to miss out on the Promised Land. Have you given place to unbelief? If so, how?

_____

_____

If God has promised you something, *it is going to happen*. The question is, will you be ready? Joseph didn't have time to get "prayed up" in order to hear from God. He had to remain ready. How are you preparing to be *ready* when God moves? What can you do to nourish and protect your dream until it is birthed?

_____

Journal the development of your dream. This record will encourage you and remind you of God's faithfulness in the future.

SESSION SUMMARY

The strongest form of resistance against the enemy is consistent obedience. When you obey God in the midst of trials, the character of Christ is carved into you. Absolute obedience is also the basis of destroying ungodly strongholds in your thinking, enabling you to rise to new levels of authority in God's Kingdom.

Notes

(1) Adapted from *Noah Webster's First Edition of an American Dictionary of the English Language* (1828), Republished in facsimile edition by Foundation for American Christian Education (San Francisco, CA 2000). (2) Christian quotes on *Trust* (retrieved 8/13/11, http://dailychristianquote.com/dcqtrust.html). (3) Adapted from: the *Life Application Bible* copyright © 1988, 1989, 1990, 1991 Tyndale House Publishers, Inc. Wheaton, IL 60189. All rights reserved. (New International Version edition; dates found in the Chronology of Bible Events and World Events, just before Genesis). New International Version edition is published jointly by Tyndale House Publishers, Inc. and Zondervan Publishing House. (4) Adapted from *The Word In Life™ Study Bible* copyright © 1993, 1996 by Thomas Nelson, Inc. Used by Permission (New King James Version, p. 80). (5) Quotes by *Kay Arthur* (retrieved 8/13/11, http://dailychristianquote.com/dcqarthur.html). (6) *Stories for the Heart*, compiled by Alice Gray (Sisters, OR: Multnomah Publishers, Inc., 1996) "Choosing," p. 66. (7) See note 1. (8) Quotes by *Amy Carmichael* (retrieved 8/13/11, http://dailychristianquote.com/dcqcarmichael.html). (9) Adapted from *Strong's Exhaustive Concordance of the Bible*, James Strong, LL.D., S.T.D. (Nashville, TN: Thomas Nelson Publishers, 1990). (10) Adapted from *Thayer's Greek-English Lexicon of the New Testament*, Joseph H. Thayer (Grand Rapids, MI: Baker Book House Company, 1977) p. 471. (11) Adapted from *Sparkling Gems from the Greek*, Rick Renner (Tulsa, OK: Teach All Nations, 2003) p. 918-919. (12) See note 9. (13) See note 10, p. 628.

The earnest (heartfelt, continued) prayer of a righteous man makes tremendous power available [dynamic in its working].

—James 5:16 AMP

Chapter 11

RELENTLESS PRAYER

Please refer to session 11 of the teaching series,
along with chapter 15 in the Relentless book.

1. Prayer is an indispensable part of living relentlessly. It is not an event. It is a way of life. This
   is why we are instructed to "pray without ceas-
   ing" in 1 Thessalonians 5:17 (NKJV). In your
   own words, briefly describe the value and
   importance of prayer in your life.

   _____

   _____

   _____

   _____

   _____

   _____

   _____

   _____

   _____

   _____

   _____

   _____

SETTING *the* PACE

"Prayer is the source of the
Christian life, a Christian's
lifeline. ...Satan's main strat-
egy with God's people has
always been to whisper,
'Don't call, don't ask, don't
depend on God to do great
things. You'll get along fine
if you just rely on your own
cleverness and energy.'
The truth of the matter is
that the devil is not terribly
frightened of our human
efforts and credentials. But
he knows his kingdom will
be damaged when we lift
up our hearts to God."
—*Jim Cymbala*[1]

PRAYER
A DEEPER UNDERSTANDING

In the New Testament, there are about eight Greek words used for prayer.
The one used most frequently is *proseuche*, appearing over 125 times. It's
derived from two words: *pros* and *euche*. *Pros* means "toward" and signifies
"a sense of closeness, intimacy and face-to-face contact."

Euche is a word describing a deep desire or wish that was joined to a vow. It originally portrayed someone who had a great need and prayed to God for the answer, vowing to give Him something of great value in return. Hannah's prayer and vow to God for a son is a perfect example of a *euche* (see 1 Samuel 1-2:11).

The other integral parts of prayer (*euche*) included giving thanks, praise, and worship.[2] With this understanding, we see that prayer is a channel of communication and intimate communion, bringing us into face-to-face contact with our heavenly Father. It expresses our love and heartfelt thanks, praise, and worship for who He is and what He has done.

G 2. We can, and should, approach God *anywhere*, *anytime*, about *anything*. Prayer is to be an ongoing, life-giving exchange between us and our heavenly Father. Carefully read these verses describing your open invitation into God's presence.

> In Whom, because of our faith in {Jesus}, we dare to have the boldness (courage and confidence) of free access (an unreserved approach to God with freedom and without fear).
>
> **—*Ephesians 3:12 AMP***

> Let us then fearlessly and confidently and boldly draw near to the throne of grace (the throne of God's unmerited favor to us sinners), that we may receive mercy [for our failures] and find grace to help in good time for every need [appropriate help and well-timed help, coming just when we need it].
>
> **—*Hebrews 4:16 AMP***

> And so, dear brothers and sisters, we can boldly enter heaven's Most Holy Place because of the blood of Jesus. By his death, Jesus opened a new and life-giving way through the curtain into the Most Holy Place. And since we have a great High Priest who rules over God's house, let us go right into the presence of God with sincere hearts fully trusting him. For our guilty consciences have been sprinkled with Christ's blood to make us clean, and our bodies have been washed with pure water.
>
> **—*Hebrews 10:19-22 NLT***
> {Word in brackets added for clarity}

How does God want you to approach Him? What gives you access to Him? What is available in His presence?

_____

_____

_____

And pray in the Spirit on all occasions with all kinds of prayers and requests.
With this in mind, be alert and always keep on praying for all the saints.
—Ephesians 6:18 NIV

G 3. Jesus knew how vital and valuable prayer is. In His Sermon on the Mount, He gave us direction about the elements our prayers should include. Slowly meditate on His words, and listen for what His Spirit reveals to you about prayer.

> "When you pray, don't babble on and on as people of other religions do. They think their prayers are answered merely by repeating their words again and again. Don't be like them, for your Father knows exactly what you need even before you ask him! Pray like this:
>
> Our Father in heaven, may your
> name be kept holy.
> May your Kingdom come soon.
> May your will be done on earth,
> as it is in heaven.
> Give us today the food we need,
> and forgive us our sins, as we have forgiven
> those who sin against us.
> And don't let us yield to temptation, but
> rescue us from the evil one."
> *—Matthew 6:7-13 NLT*

What principles of prayer is the Holy Spirit showing you in Jesus' words?

_____

_____

_____

_____

4. Since prayer is communion with the Lord, it involves talking and *listening*. God is speaking to you, and you can hear Him. Carefully meditate on these verses.

> But the gatekeeper opens the gate for the shepherd, and he goes in through it. The sheep know their shepherd's voice. He calls each of them by name and leads them out. When he has led out all of his sheep, he walks in front of them, and they follow, because they know his voice. The

SETTING *the* PACE

"Prayer is not just an activity, a ritual, or an obligation. Nor is it begging God to do what we want Him to do. It is *communion* and *communication* with God that touches His heart. When you understand the principles of the art of prayer, you will begin to communicate with God with power, grace and confidence. Prayer is meant to be one of the most exciting aspects of a life of faith. It has the power to transform lives, change circumstances, give peace and perseverance in the midst of trial, alter the course of nations, and win the world for Christ. The power of prayer is the inheritance of the believer."
—Dr. Myles Munroe[3]

sheep will not follow strangers. They don't recognize a stranger's voice, and they run away.

—John 10:2-5 CEV

I am the good shepherd; I know my own sheep, and they know me, just as my Father knows me and I know the Father. So I sacrifice my life for the sheep. I have other sheep, too, that are not in this sheepfold. I must bring them also. They will listen to my voice, and there will be one flock with one shepherd. (NLT) My sheep hear My voice, and I know them, and they follow Me. (NKJV)

—John 10:14-16, 27

You have given me the capacity to hear and obey [Your law, a more valuable service than] burnt offerings and sin offerings [which] You do not require.

—Psalm 40:6 AMP

And if you leave God's paths and go astray, you will hear a Voice behind you say, "No, this is the way; walk here."

—Isaiah 30:21 TLB

What is the Holy Spirit showing you about being able to hear His voice?

_____

_____

_____

Group leader extra: God promises to guide us in Psalm 25:9, 12-14; 32:8; 48:14 and Matthew 28:20.

CORE STRENGTHENER

Our objective is not frequent speaking in prayer; it is a determination to receive. The focus is a relentless, fervent, and sure attitude in making our requests. We approach God confidently because we know our request is according to His will, and consequently we will not be denied.

5. In order to fervently and earnestly pray for God's answer in a situation, we must know *His will* regarding it. Knowing God's will comes from knowing His Word and knowing what His Spirit speaks to us that is confirmed in His Word. Slowly read these scriptures.

But if you remain in me and my words remain in you, you may ask for anything you want, and it will be granted!

—John 15:7 NLT

And this is the confidence (the assurance, the privilege of boldness) which we have in Him: [we are sure] that if we ask anything (make any request) according to His will (in agreement with His own plan), He listens to and hears us. And if (since) we [positively] know that He listens to us in whatever we ask, we also know [with settled and absolute knowledge] that we have [granted us as our present possessions] the requests made of Him.

—1 John 5:14-15 AMP

You can ask him for anything, using my name, and I will do it, for this will bring praise to the Father because of what I, the Son, will do for you. Yes, ask anything, using my name, and I will do it!

—*John 14:13-14 TLB*

Why is it important to know God's will? What can you be sure of once you know it?

_____

_____

_____

I delight to do Your will, O my God; yes, Your law is within my heart. Teach me to do Your will, for You are my God; let Your good Spirit lead me into a level country and into the land of uprightness.
—Psalm 40:8; 143:10 AMP

EFFECTUAL and FERVENT

The word *effectual* is the Greek word *energeo*. It means "to be active, operative and mighty effective in its work."[4] Webster defines *effectual* as "producing the desired or intended effect; having adequate power or force to produce the effect; veracious (truthful, honest)."[5]

The word *fervent* is the Greek word *zeo*, meaning "to be hot, to boil." It is where we get the word *zeal* from.[6] The phrase *fervent prayer* in the King James Version is actually from one Greek expression, *deisis*. It means "a passionate, earnest, heartfelt, sincere prayer" that is lifted up to God on very serious terms, pleading with Him to meet a specific need.[7]

G ☐ 6. There is a big difference between *wishing* to receive something from God and being *determined* to receive. When we're determined, we pray fervently. Carefully read the story of the widow and the unjust judge in Luke 18:1-8. Notice that Jesus says we are to learn from the unjust *judge*, not from the widow. What does this speak to you about your approach to prayer?

_____

_____

_____

_____

So I say to you, Ask and keep on asking and it shall be given you; seek and keep on seeking and you shall find; knock and keep on knocking and the door shall be opened to you. For everyone who asks and keeps

CORE STRENGTHENER

We must always remember that God "is able to do exceedingly abundantly above all that we ask or think, according to the power that works in us" (Ephesians 3:20 NKJV). We cannot allow our finite, human minds to limit Him in our thinking and believing. If we really believe, we'll ask persistently and keep knocking until we see His glory revealed.

SETTING the PACE

"When times get tough, it's tempting to neglect the secret place. Jesus, however, manifested precisely the opposite tendency. When He was hurting, He sought out the place of prayer. His time in Gethsemane is a great example of this... (Luke 22:44). When Jesus was hurting, He prayed. When He hurt real hard, He prayed even harder. *This was Jesus' secret to enduring the horror of His sufferings. He prepared Himself through prayer to endure the pain.* If we respond properly, distress can actually be a gift. Pain can provide tremendous impetus to pray—if we will allow it to catapult us into God's face instead of polarizing us away from Him."
—Bob Sorge[8]

on asking receives; and he who seeks and keeps on seeking finds; and to him who knocks and keeps on knocking, the door shall be opened.
—Luke 11:9-10 AMP

7. When Elijah fervently prayed for rain, God confirmed it was on the way by sending a small cloud as a sign. Today, we're not looking for a physical cloud to confirm our prayers are answered. We're awaiting a confirmation from the Holy Spirit. Describe some of the ways God's Spirit has confirmed your prayers were answered. Were you ever tempted to let go of the confirmation God gave you? If so, explain how you responded.

_____

_____

_____

_____

_____

8. Have you prayed and prayed for God to move in a certain situation without seeming to see a change? If so, briefly describe the situation. How does the story of Elijah praying for rain *seven times* before he received an answer encourage and motivate you to set your face like flint in your petitions?

_____

_____

_____

_____

_____

Group leader extra: Read Elijah's story in 1 Kings 18:41-45 and James 5:17-18.

*For the Lord God helps Me; therefore have I not been ashamed or confounded. Therefore have **I set My face like a flint**, and I know that I shall not be put to shame.*
—Isaiah 50:7 AMP

9. Fervent prayer is effective and birthed out of great passion. Stop and ask yourself: *What is burning in my heart? What injustice or ungodly activity in my life or the lives of those around me do I passionately want to see changed? Who or what does God want me to earnestly intercede for in prayer?* Get quiet before Him and ask Him for discernment. Write what He speaks to you.

God wants me to fervently pray for:

_____

_____

_____

_____

_____

10. Has God given you an idea to bring Him glory that seems like an insurmountable task? Is it connected with the dream you wrote about in chapter 10? Briefly share your idea. Pray and ask God to confirm that it's from Him. If He does, ask Him for His grace and any specific actions He wants you to take toward it.

The idea God has placed in my heart is...

_____

_____

_____

_____

_____

The actions I am to take to see it become a reality are...

_____

_____

_____

_____

_____

_____

SETTING *the* PACE

"When we pray for someone, we *intercede*. That means we mentally get involved in their world as we deliberately make contact with God on their behalf. This, admittedly, is only one aspect of prayer, but it's a mighty important one! ...There is no more significant involvement in another's life than prevailing, consistent prayer. It is more helpful than a gift of money, more encouraging than a strong sermon, more effective than a compliment, more reassuring than a physical embrace."
—*Charles R. Swindoll*[9]

CORE STRENGTHENER

Don't be shy in approaching God—don't be timid with your requests. Be bold, strong, adamant and specific. Our persistence with God does not come from desperation, but from confidence that He is our loving Father and will give us what we adamantly ask for in His name. What are you waiting for? The needs around you are great. There are so many people in your world who need you to approach God boldly in prayer on their behalf. Be a light to them! Approach God with relentless persistence now!

Weekly
CHALLENGE

In a notebook or journal, begin recording your prayers and the answers to them. In one column, write your requests and the dates that you begin interceding for them. Fervently claim the promises of God over each situation until the answer manifests. In a second column, record the day and manner in which the fulfillment occurs. Commitment and reflection will enable you to persevere in your prayers and celebrate the way God moves through them. Keep this journal for at least 30 days.

Example

My Request	God's Response
February 12 – A full-time job. Needed within next two weeks. Philippians 4:19, Matthew 6:25-34	*February 20 – Job offer from advertising firm!*

Day 1 CREATING THE CONDITIONS FOR SUCCESSFUL PRAYER

Hear my cry, O God; listen to my prayer.

—Psalm 61:1 AMP

All of us want our prayers to be successful, for God to hear and answer us when we call. Scripture clearly identifies keys to answered and unanswered prayers. Although this list is not exhaustive, it will remind you of things you have forgotten and open your eyes to new truths.

What are the **conditions of successful prayer** found in these Scriptures?

2 Chronicles 7:14 _____

Psalm 34:11-18 _____

Psalm 91:14-15 _____

Jeremiah 29:12-13 _____

Matthew 21:21-22; Mark 11:24 _____

John 15:7; 1 John 3:21-24 _____

Which attributes are operating in your life? How can you develop the others?

_____

_____

Sometimes the answer to our prayer appears to be *delayed. Read* Daniel 10:10-14 and John 11:1-6 and identify two reasons for delayed answers.

_____

What are the common **causes for unanswered prayer** in these Scriptures?

Psalm 66:18; Isaiah 59:1-2 _____

Proverbs 21:13 _____

Proverbs 1:28-31; 28:9 _____

Mark 11:25: Matthew 5:23-24 _____

Mark 6:5-6; James 1:6-7 _____

James 4:3 _____

Get quiet before the Lord. Ask Him if any of these are at work in your life. Repent and ask for grace to take the action He directs. Write what He reveals.

_____

_____

Day 2 **THE POWER OF WORSHIP**

*"**Worship the Lord your God**, and only him. Serve him with absolute single-heartedness."*

—Matthew 4:10 The Message

Prayer and worship are inseparable. The definitions of the two most common Greek words for prayer include *worship*.[10] Worship is much more than singing. Jesus said, "It's who you are and the way you live that count before God. Your worship must engage your spirit in the pursuit of truth. That's the kind of people the Father is out looking for: those who are simply and honestly themselves before him in their worship. God is sheer being itself—Spirit. Those who worship him must do it out of their very being, their spirits, their true selves, in adoration" (John 4:23-24 The Message).

WORSHIP

The word *worship* in the New Testament is almost always the Greek word *proskuneo*, a compound of *pros* and *kueno*. *Pros*, which is also used to form the word prayer, means "toward" and signifies "a sense of face-to-face intimacy." *Kuneo* means "to kiss."[11] Putting the two words together, they mean "to prostrate oneself in homage, reverence or adoration."[12] *Worship* means to honor, adore, give extravagant love and submission to.[13]

Webster explains that *worship* is derived from *worth* and *ship*. To worship God is to see Him as *having great worth* and express appreciation with our words of thanks and praise, our deeds, and our lives.

How do you express your appreciation to God? How does He express His love for you? If you don't take time to worship, why?

_____

_____

When someone sincerely praises your work or character, adding worth and value to who you are, how does it make you feel? How does it make you feel about that person? How do you think God feels when you worship Him?

_____

_____

Read Acts 16:23-40. List the manifestations of God's power as a result of Paul and Silas' worship in the midst of suffering. What does this say to you?

_____

_____

Day 3 THE POWER OF PRAYING IN JESUS' NAME

For this reason also, God...bestowed on Him the name which is above every name, so that at the name of Jesus every knee will bow.
—Philippians 2:9-10 NASB

The name of Jesus is a mighty weapon. Everything—absolutely everything—that is promised in Scripture comes to us because of that name! This is the name above every name, "and there is salvation in no one else; for there is no other name under heaven...by which we must be saved" (Acts 4:12 NASB).

Meditate on the message of these amazing promises from Jesus:
My Father will give you whatever you ask for *in my name.*
—*John 15:16 CEV*

This is what I want you to do: Ask the Father for whatever is in keeping with the things I've revealed to you. Ask *in my name*, according to my will, and he'll most certainly give it to you. Your joy will be a river overflowing its banks!
—*John 16:23-24 The Message*

I tell you the truth, anyone who believes in me will do the same works I have done, and even greater works, because I am going to be with the Father. Yes, ask me for anything *in my name*, and I will do it!
—*John 14:12, 14 NLT*

What is the Holy Spirit speaking about praying in the name of Jesus?

_____

Read Acts 2:38, 4:11-12, 10:43; Luke 24:47 and 1 John 2:12. What do these verses repeatedly declare is yours and all mankind's through the name of Jesus?

_____

_____

Read John 1:12 and 20:31. What blessings do these verses reveal are yours in Jesus' name?

_____

_____

Read what God did through Peter and John in Acts 3:1-10, 16 and how the Sanhedrin responded in Acts 4:17-18. What does this say to you about the power of Jesus' name?

_____

_____

Day 4 THE POWER OF PRAYING GOD'S WORD

His powerful Word is sharp as a surgeon's scalpel, cutting through everything,
whether doubt or defense, laying us open to listen and obey. Nothing and no one
is impervious to God's Word. We can't get away from it—no matter what.
—Hebrews 4:12-13 The Message

God's Word is alive! His Word is life! (John 6:63; Deuteronomy 32:45-47) What did He use to create the world? *The Word* (John 1:1-3). What did He send to redeem mankind? *The Word* (John 1:14). What did Jesus give us to save and sanctify us? *The Word* (Psalm 138:2).

Meditate on the message of these scriptures:
No word from God shall be without power or impossible of fulfillment.
—Luke 1:37 AMP

Then the Lord said to me, "You have seen well, for I am watching over My word to perform it."

—Jeremiah 1:12 NASB

Bless the Lord, you His angels, who excel in strength, who do His word, heeding the voice of His word.

—Psalm 103:20 NKJV

What has God Himself promised in Jeremiah 1:12 to do regarding His Word? What does this speak to you?

_____

_____

How do the invisible, yet powerful, angelic forces of heaven respond to God's Word? See Hebrews 1:14.

_____

The question is *do you believe this*? If so, how do these truths excite you? If you don't believe this, why? Ask God to show you what's short-circuiting your faith. Release it to Him and meditate on Numbers 23:19.

_____

_____

"My word, which comes from my mouth, is like the rain and snow.
It will not come back to me without results, but it will accomplish
whatever I want and achieve whatever I send it to do."
—Isaiah 55:11 GW

Day 5 THE POWER OF THE BLOOD OF JESUS

*Our people defeated Satan because of the **blood of the Lamb** and the message of God. They were willing to give up their lives.*

—Revelation 12:11 CEV

The blood of Jesus Christ is powerful! Through faith in Him—believing He paid the penalty for our sins—we are justified and *saved from God's wrath* (see Romans 5:9). His blood doesn't just cover up sins like the sacrifices of bulls and goats. His blood *takes our sin away* once and for all (see Hebrews 10:4, 11-12). It *cleanses our consciences* continually as we abide in Him (see Hebrews 9:14; 1 John 1:7). Through His blood we can confidently *enter God's presence* in prayer (see Hebrews 10:19). Praise God for the precious blood of Jesus!

Fascinating Facts About Blood
- The human body contains about *5 quarts* of blood.
- Every cell is constantly *nourished* and *cleansed* by the blood. If blood stops flowing, life stops flowing.
- The two main components of blood are *red blood cells* and *white blood cells*.
  - White blood cells *protect the body* by destroying disease.
  - Red blood cells carry *oxygen* and *food* to cells.
- Blood cells *pick up the waste products* of each cell, eventually disposing of them.
- Five quarts of blood circulate in our system every *23 seconds*.[14]

Carefully reread the facts about blood. What parallels can you see with the blood of Jesus, which is spiritually at work within us—the Body of Christ?

_____

_____

Read Exodus 12:1-13. What the Israelites did physically, we are to do spiritually by faith. **Write out a prayer**, putting the blood of Jesus over you, your children, your home, your finances, and everything He has made you steward of.

_____

_____

Think about this: Would there be any power in Jesus' name without His shed blood? Would there be any power in praying God's Word without His blood? Would there be any power in the armor of God without His blood? Slowly reread the opening paragraph and **write a prayer of thanksgiving and praise** for Jesus Christ shedding His blood for you.

_____

_____

_____

Day 6 THE POWER OF PRAYING IN THE SPIRIT

But you, my friends, keep on building yourselves up on your most sacred faith.
Pray in the power of the Holy Spirit.

—Jude 1:20 GNT

When we accept God's free gift of salvation through Jesus Christ His Son, we are immediately born again and placed into His Kingdom. The Spirit of God the Father and of Christ comes to live inside us (see John 14:23). The first time this took place was just after Jesus' resurrection when He appeared to His disciples behind locked doors. John 20:21-22 records, "Jesus said, 'Peace be with you! As the Father has sent me, I am sending you.' And with that he breathed on them and said, 'Receive the Holy Spirit'" (NIV).

Before He ascended into heaven, Jesus commanded these same disciples to wait in Jerusalem for the gift of the baptism of the Holy Spirit (see Acts 1:4-5, 8). Jesus says the baptism of the Spirit is being **clothed with power** (see Luke 24:49 NIV). Yes, the Holy Spirit was living in them, but the baptism of the Spirit is distinctly different (see Acts 8:12-17). It is a greater manifestation of God's supreme, powerful rule. To be Jesus' witnesses in a hostile world, His disciples needed this total immersion in His Spirit. The same holds true for us today.

Who is the Holy Spirit to you?
He is your **Comforter, Counselor,** and **Truth detector**.......John 14:16-17, 15:26, 16:7-15
He is your **Teacher**..................Matthew 10:19-20; Luke 12:11-12; John 14:26; 1 John 2:27
He is your **Source of Grace**..Hebrews 10:29
He is your **Guide**..............................Acts 10:19-20, 13:2; Romans 8:14; Galatians 5:16-26
He is your **Life-Giver**..............................John 6:63; Romans 8:2, 6, 11; 2 Corinthians 3:6
He is your **Power**..Luke 24:49; Acts 1:8

What evidence did Jesus say would accompany this powerful infilling? To whom is it promised? *Read* Mark 16:17; Acts 2:4, 38-39; 10:44-46 and 19:3-6.

_____

_____

_____

Before the disciples were baptized in the Holy Spirit on the day of Pentecost, they hid behind closed doors. What effect did being *clothed with power* have on them? What effect will He have on you? *Read* Acts 4:8-13, 31-35 and 5:27-42.

_____

_____

_____

_____

When you need to pray during trials, how does the Holy Spirit help you? *Read* Romans 8:26-27.

_____

_____

_____

_____

The gift of the baptism of the Holy Spirit is an *ongoing infilling*, not a one-time event. This is why Paul says, "**Ever be filled** and stimulated with the [Holy] Spirit," and why Jude tells us to "**keep on** building yourselves up on your most sacred faith. Pray in the power of the Holy Spirit" (Ephesians 5:18 AMP; Jude 1:20 GNT).

Have you received the gift of the baptism of the Holy Spirit? If not, *would you like to*? All you have to do is ask. Jesus said, "...Your heavenly Father is even more ready to give the Holy Spirit to anyone who asks" (Luke 11:13 CEV). Once you ask for the Holy Spirit, you will *receive* the Holy Spirit. Acts 2:4 says, "And they were all filled with the Holy Spirit and began to speak with other tongues, as the Spirit gave them utterance" (NKJV). The word *utterance* means "syllables, sounds, or words." After you pray, you will probably sense a syllable, sound or word bubbling up inside of you. Although the impression may be faint and you may feel silly, *speak it out*! The Holy Spirit is giving you the utterance, but you must *yield* your lips, tongue, and vocal cords to speak what He is impressing upon you.

Are you ready to receive? Do you believe you will have what you ask for? Are you willing to yield yourself to the Holy Spirit? Then pray...

Prayer for the Promised Gift of the Holy Spirit

Father, I come to You in the name of Jesus. First of all, I repent of any sin that would hinder me from receiving from You, including the sin of unforgiveness. By Your grace and as an act of my will, I release anyone who has offended me and bless them with all Your best; I thank you that I am cleansed with the blood of Jesus.

Now, as Your child, I ask You for the promised gift of the Holy Spirit. You said if I ask You for the Holy Spirit, You will give Him to me, so by faith I ask You now to baptize me with Your Holy Spirit. I receive everything You have for me, including the ability to speak in a new heavenly language. Now in faith, I will speak in new tongues in Jesus' name!

SESSION SUMMARY

Prayer is your lifeline of communication and communion with the Lord. It is not hampered by place or posture. You can lift up your voice anytime, anywhere, about anything. All that is required is a humble heart. Relentless prayer is fervent and effective, releasing dynamic power into your situations. When circumstances arise in your life that are contrary to God's will, press in to God's presence; keep on asking, seeking, and knocking until the answer you need is confirmed by His Spirit.

(1) Jim Cymbala, *Fresh Wind, Fresh Fire* (Grand Rapids, MI: Zondervan Publishing House, 1997) pp. 50, 56. (2) Adapted from *Sparkling Gems from the Greek*, Rick Renner (Tulsa, OK: Teach All Nations, 2003) pp. 334-335. (3) Dr. Myles Munroe, *Understanding the Purpose and Power of Prayer* (New Kensington, PA: Whitaker House, 2002) pp. 22-23. (4) Adapted from *Strong's Exhaustive Concordance of the Bible*, James Strong, LL.D., S.T.D. (Nashville, TN: Thomas Nelson Publishers, 1990). (5) Adapted from *Noah Webster's First Edition of an American Dictionary of the English Language* (1828), Republished in facsimile edition by Foundation for American Christian Education (San Francisco, CA 2000). (6) Adapted from *Vine's Complete Expository Dictionary of Old and New Testament Words*, W.E. Vine (Nashville, TN: Thomas Nelson Publishing, 1996) p. 233. (7) See note 2, p. 710. (8) Bob Sorge, *Secrets of the Secret Place* (Greenwood, MO: Oasis House, 2001) p. 122. (9) Charles R. Swindoll, *The Quest for Character* (Portland, OR: Multnomah Press, 1987) pp. 130, 132. (10) See note 4. (11) See note 6, p. 686. (12) See note 4. (13) See note 5. (14) Adapted from *The Word, The Name, The Blood*, Joyce Meyer (New York, NY: Warner Faith, 2003) pp. 133-134.

Notes

Never give up. *Eagerly follow the Holy Spirit and serve the Lord. Let your hope make you glad. Be patient in time of trouble and never stop praying.*

—Romans 12:11-12 CEV

12

NEVER GIVE UP

Please refer to session 12 of the teaching series, along with chapters 16, 17 and 18 in the Relentless book.

G 1. Jesus said in the last days, many will give up and turn away from their faith in Him. Persecution and tribulation will increase, and those who have a wrong perspective of it will not be armed to suffer and will fall away (see Matthew 24:9-10; 1 Peter 4:1). What is your perspective toward suffering and trials? How has it changed since you began this study?

_____

_____

_____

_____

_____

2. Quitting manifests in different forms, but most often as *compromise*: going a little below the standard of what we know is right. Does this describe you? Are you compromising in any area of your thinking, speaking, or acting? *Get quiet before God.* Ask Him to show you your heart. Write what He reveals, including any actions He prompts you to take.

_____

_____

_____

_____

_____

CORE STRENGTHENER

No one can force you to quit. God certainly won't and the devil can't. You are the only one who makes that decision. So don't quit! The reward for overcoming, both in this life and the next, is far greater than the adversity or hardship you face.

SETTING *the* PACE

"*Get God's viewpoint.* Do what the Word of God tells you to do. Follow the promptings of the Holy Spirit. And you will know how to walk wisely. Determine in your heart that you will trust God day by day. Persevere in what God directs you to do. And you will walk in wisdom...all the way to eternity's door."

—Charles Stanley[1]

179

Don't quit. Don't cave in. It is all well worth it in the end.
—Matthew 10:22 The Message

G 3. Many who profess to be Christians today are reshaping Scripture to accommodate the trends in society instead of allowing the truth of Scripture to shape them. In other words, they're *reading into* God's Word what they want it to say instead of *drawing out of it* what it actually says. Why is this dangerous? How can you guard against it?

LAWLESSNESS and LASCIVIOUSNESS

Lawlessness (translated iniquity in the KJV) is "the condition of one without law—either because of ignorance or violation; contempt (disrespect, hatred) for the law."[2] Webster defines it as "the quality or state of being unrestrained by law; disorder.[3]

Lasciviousness means "looseness; irregular indulgence of animal desires; lustfulness and wantonness, which means excessive and unrestrained."[4] In Scripture, *lascivious* also signifies "unbridled lust, excess, shamelessness, outrageousness, filthy conversation and licentiousness (decadence, immorality)."[5] Lawlessness and lasciviousness are used repeatedly in Scripture to describe the condition of not only the world, but also *the church* in the last days.

G 4. The biggest problem in the early church was legalism. The biggest problem we are facing in the church in these last days is *lawlessness* and *lasciviousness*. This is what makes it so difficult to be a Christian. What is the root reason for this type of lifestyle among people claiming to be believers? What danger does this trend communicate?

The root reason for lawlessness and lasciviousness among Christians is...

The danger this trend communicates is...

G 5. Jesus compared the time before His return to the *days of Noah* and the *days of Lot*. Both men are considered followers of God, but there were definite differences in their characters and ways of life. What are those differences? Which man do you most identify with? Why?

SETTING *the* **PACE**

"Christianity will always reproduce itself after its kind. A worldly-minded, unspiritual church...is sure to bring forth on other shores a Christianity much like her own. Not the naked Word only but the charac-ter of the witness deter-mines the quality of the convert. The church can do no more than transplant herself. What she is in one land she will be in another."
—*A.W. Tozer*[6]

Noah's Character and Lifestyle Genesis 6:1-7:5, 8:15-22	Lot's Character and Lifestyle Genesis 13:10-13, 19:1-38

I most identify with _____ because...

Group leader extra: Jesus refers to the days of Noah and Lot in Matthew 24:36-39 and Luke 17:26-33.

We are pressed on every side by troubles, but not crushed and broken. We are perplexed because we don't know why things happen as they do, but we don't give up and quit. We are hunted down, but God never abandons us. We get knocked down, but we get up again and keep going.
—2 Corinthians 4:8-9 TLB

G 6. God doesn't want you to feel overwhelmed about being a Christian in these last days. Instead, He wants you to draw close to Him, receive His grace, and gain a greater understanding of His keeping power.

Meditate on the message of these amazing promises.
Now all glory to God, who is able to keep you from falling away and will bring you with great joy into his glorious presence without a single fault.
—*Jude 1:24 NLT*

The Lord is your keeper; the Lord is your shade on your right hand [the side not carrying a shield]. The sun shall not smite you by day, nor the moon by night. The Lord will keep you from all evil; He will keep your life. The Lord will keep your going out and your coming in from this time forth and forevermore.
—*Psalm 121:5-8 AMP*

Since the day you were born, I have carried you along. I will still be the same when you are old and gray, and I will take care of you. I created you. I will carry you and always keep you safe. Can anyone compare with me? Is anyone my equal?

—Isaiah 46:3-5 CEV

God the Father has his eye on each of you, and has determined by the work of the Spirit to keep you obedient through the sacrifice of Jesus. May everything good from God be yours!

—1 Peter 1:2 The Message

What new insights is the Lord showing you about His ability to keep you?

_____

_____

_____

_____

*May God himself, the God who makes everything holy and whole,
make you holy and whole, put you together—spirit, soul, and body—and
keep you fit for the coming of our Master, Jesus Christ. The One
who called you is completely dependable. If he said it, he'll do it!*
—1 Thessalonians 5:23-24 The Message

7.   While God promises to keep us, there is something we must do. Carefully read these verses and identify your part in ensuring God's protection. How does it relate to what you have already learned in this study?

Because you have guarded and kept My word of patient endurance [have held fast the lesson of My patience with the expectant endurance that I give you], I also will keep you [safe] from the hour of trial (testing) which is coming on the whole world to try those who dwell upon the earth. I am coming quickly; hold fast what you have, so that no one may rob you and deprive you of your crown.

—Revelation 3:10-11 AMP

I will rescue you from those you fear so much. Because you trusted me, I will give you your life as a reward. I will rescue you and keep you safe. I, the Lord, have spoken!

—Jeremiah 39:17-18 NLT

I am [positively] persuaded that He is able to guard and keep that which has been entrusted to me and which I have committed [to Him] until that day. Hold fast and follow the pattern of wholesome and sound teaching which you have heard from me, in [all] the faith and love which are [for us] in Christ Jesus.

—2 Timothy 1:12-13 AMP

My part in securing God's keeping power is...

_____

_____

_____

_____

_____

_____

_____

_____

G 8. One of the greatest motivators to never give up is knowing that God will never give up on you. He has promised to **strengthen** and **empower** you until the day your destiny is fulfilled. Carefully consider these verses from God's Word.

Now you have every spiritual gift you need as you eagerly wait for the return of our Lord Jesus Christ. *He will keep you strong to the end* so that you will be free from all blame on the day when our Lord Jesus Christ returns. God will do this, for he is faithful to do what he says, and he has invited you into partnership with his Son, Jesus Christ our Lord.

—1 Corinthians 1:7-9 NLT

I have strength for all things in Christ Who empowers me [I am ready for anything and equal to anything through Him Who *infuses inner strength into me*; I am self-sufficient in Christ's sufficiency].

—Philippians 4:13 AMP

God doesn't come and go. God lasts. He's Creator of all you can see or imagine. He doesn't get tired out, doesn't pause to catch his breath. And he knows everything, inside and out. *He energizes those who get tired, gives fresh strength* to dropouts. For even young people tire and drop out, young folk in their prime stumble and fall. But those who wait upon God get fresh strength. They spread their wings and soar like eagles, they run and don't get tired, they walk and don't lag behind.

—Isaiah 40:28-31 The Message

I pray that from his glorious, unlimited resources *he will empower you with inner strength* through his Spirit. Then Christ will make his home in your hearts as you trust in him. Your roots will grow down into God's love and keep you strong. And may you have the power to understand, as all God's people should, how wide, how long, how high, and how deep his love is.

—Ephesians 3:16-18 NLT

How do these truths encourage you to believe God for strength? Again, what is your part?

_____

_____

_____

CORE STRENGTHENER

God has given you the faith to get through every hardship and adversity you will face. Run relentlessly the race set before you, confidently fighting any opposition to the end. You are an overcomer. You possess the seed of the one who endured the greatest opposition ever encountered. His strength is in you! His nature is yours. You were not made to quit, draw back, falter, or compromise. You've been blessed with the amazing grace of God. No matter how great the adversity against you, view it as a steppingstone to the next level of rulership.

9. Just after Paul urges us to *continue in the truth of Scripture* in order to not fall away from the faith and reject the grace of God, He gives us an urgent charge. Slowly read through his words, taking them personally to heart as if God Himself is saying them to you.

I charge [you] in the presence of God and of Christ Jesus, Who is to judge the living and the dead, and by (in the light of) His coming and His kingdom: *Herald and preach the Word!* Keep your sense of urgency [stand by, be at hand and ready], whether the opportunity seems to be favorable or unfavorable. [Whether it is convenient or inconvenient, whether it is welcome or unwelcome, you as preacher of the Word are to show people in what way their lives are wrong.] And convince them, rebuking and correcting, warning and urging and encouraging them, being unflagging and inexhaustible in patience and teaching.

—*2 Timothy 4:1-2 AMP*

What is God speaking to you personally through this charge? How does it motivate you?

_____

_____

_____

10. As we come to the end of this study, stop and ask yourself this vital question: *Am I living relentlessly, or have I given up? Am I really pressing toward the high calling God has for my life, or am I just putting up a good front?* Get quiet before the Lord and ask Him to search your heart and show you where you stand. If you have given up or reduced your forward momentum, ask Him to show you why. Write what He speaks to your heart.

_____

_____

_____

_____

_____

_____

_____

_____

Stay with God! Take heart. Don't quit.
I'll say it again: Stay with God.
—Psalm 27:14 The Message

Prayer

Father, thank You for teaching me in this study. It is my heart's desire to live relentlessly for You and never give up. Please give me Your grace daily to persevere and live for You. Help me to continue in the truth of Your Word and not give in to compromise. May I be a blazing flame of Your love, peace, and power in the earth. Live through me, Holy Spirit. Help me hear Your voice and obediently follow You. Help me be ready at all times to be Your witness and to be ready for Your return. In Jesus' name, Amen.

Weekly CHALLENGE

SETTING *the* PACE

"Here are the reps that will guide you toward perfect execution of the Christian life. The first drill is to study your Bible reflectively each day. The second is to be a person of prayer—regular and disciplined. Do these things over and over, for every situation. There will be days you don't feel like doing these things. ...But those hard-nosed decisions to be consistent will separate you from the lukewarm faith crowd. They will cause you to experience Christ in ways you never could have anticipated. *Read, pray, serve, repeat.* Do this every day, and on that wondrous day when Christ returns, you will stand before Him without shame."

—*David Jeremiah*[8]

A generation of uncompromising champions is destined to arise in the Church of our day. A company of believers is meant not only to fellowship and share in the joy of salvation together but also to confront deception and encourage steadfastness in the body of Christ. Join or lead a group of people that sharpen and strengthen each another in the power and authority of God's grace. Use this study and others like it as tools to partner with the work of the Spirit in sanctifying and empowering His children.

Let us think of ways to motivate one another to acts of love and
good works. And let us not neglect our meeting together,
as some people do, but encourage one another,
especially now that the day of his return is drawing near.
—Hebrews 10:24-25 NLT

Day 1 CONTINUE IN THE TRUTH

For your love is ever before me, and I walk continually in your truth.
—Psalm 26:3 NIV

Many believers want to know when Christ will return. Interestingly, before He told His disciples about His return, Jesus gave them a powerful warning: "Watch out that no one deceives you" (Matthew 24:4 NIV; see also Mark 13:5, Luke 21:8).

Deception abounds in these last days. To stay free from the disease of deception and never give up, we must *continue in the truth*. The importance of God's Word has been woven throughout this study. God's Word is forever established in heaven, and it will never change. It contains inherent power to save your soul, guard your heart, and set you free from ungodly, carnal thinking.

Carefully meditate on these powerful scriptures.

Stick with what you learned and believed... There's nothing like the written Word of God for showing you the way to salvation through faith in Christ Jesus. Every part of Scripture is God-breathed and useful one way or another—showing us truth, exposing our rebellion, correcting our mistakes, training us to live God's way. Through the Word we are put together and shaped up for the tasks God has for us.
—*2 Timothy 3:14-17 The Message*

The prophetic Word was confirmed to us. You'll do well to *keep focusing on it*. It's the one light you have in a dark time.
—*2 Peter 1:19 The Message*

CORE STRENGTHENER

Truth is not trendy. It remains constant through time and unaffected by culture. The alluring enticement is to follow the trends, but they only lead to deception. The antidote for following ungodly trends is to continue in the truth of God's Word.

Just as you accepted Christ Jesus as your Lord, you must continue to follow him. Let your roots grow down into him, and let your lives be built on him. Then your faith will *grow strong in the truth* you were taught.
—*Colossians 2:6-7 NLT*

How will continuing in God's Word protect you from deception and compromise?

_____

Do you remember your plan of action to saturate yourself in God's Word? If not, turn back to chapter 4 and review it. What is working for you? What is *not* working? Rewrite your plan, making any adjustments the Holy Spirit is showing you.

My plan to continue in God's Word is...

_____

_____

Day 2 BE READY AT ALL TIMES

*You also must **be ready all the time**, for the Son of Man will come when least expected.*

—Matthew 24:44 NLT

After Jesus tells His disciples to guard against deception, He tells them to *be ready at all times* for His return. This too is for us, His present-day disciples. Repeatedly we are told that He will return *like a thief* in the night (see Matthew 24:43, 1 Thessalonians 5:2-4, 2 Peter 3:10, and Revelation 3:3 and 16:15).

Read the parable of the ten virgins in Matthew 25:1-13.

What did the foolish and wise virgins have in common? What made the wise different?

_____

_____

What can you learn from this parable to apply in your life?

_____

_____

> *"Let us rejoice and be glad and give him glory! For the wedding of the Lamb has come, and his bride has made herself ready."*
> —Revelation 19:7 NIV

In addition to being ready for His return, we're also to be ready to *be His witnesses*. First Peter 3:15 in The Message says, "Keep your hearts at attention, in adoration before Christ, your Master. **Be ready to speak up** and tell anyone who asks why you're living the way you are, and always with the utmost courtesy."

If you had just a few minutes to "speak up" and share with someone in your neighborhood, at work, or in your community why you live the way you do, what would you say? Take a few minutes to sum up your testimony so that you will be ready to share. **The reason I follow Jesus Christ is...**

_____

_____

_____

_____

_____

_____

Day 3 BE BUSY DOING GOD'S WORK

We must...be busy with His business while it is daylight.

—John 9:4 AMP

As you continue in truth, you will be ready for Christ's return and ready to be His witness. Being His witness also includes doing what He has called and equipped you to do to advance His Kingdom and bring Him glory. Jesus says, "Blessings on you if I return and find you faithfully doing your work. I will put such faithful ones in charge of everything I own!" (Matthew 24:46-47 TLB).

Carefully read the *parable of the talents* in Matthew 25:14-30.

In a practical sense, what do these talents represent in your life?

_____

_____

The master gave *different amounts* of talents. What does this say to you?

_____

_____

Contrast the heart motivation of the servants who were given five or two talents with the one who received one talent. Who do you identify with?

_____

_____

How does the master's return and action of settling his accounts challenge you?

_____

_____

Related scriptures: Romans 12:5-8, 14:12

God has given each of you a gift from his great variety of spiritual gifts. Use them well to serve one another. Do you have the gift of speaking? Then speak as though God himself were speaking through you. Do you have the gift of helping others? Do it with all the strength and energy that God supplies. Then everything you do will bring glory to God through Jesus Christ.
—1 Peter 4:10-11 NLT

Read **what Jesus says right after this parable in Matthew 25:31-46.**
In what everyday, practical ways can you be busy doing God's work?

_____

_____

Day 4 KEEP YOURSELF IN GOD'S LOVE

*Keep yourselves in God's love as you wait for the mercy of our Lord Jesus Christ
to bring you to eternal life.*

—Jude 1:21 NIV

Jesus says in the last days "evil will spread and cause many people to *stop loving others.* But if you keep on being faithful right to the end, you will be saved"
(Matthew 24:12-13 CEV). A key to being faithful is to keep yourself in God's love.

To walk in love is not a suggestion: it is a command. It is an aspect of true
humility, as we learned in session 7. Love is not something God does. It's who
he is (1 John 4:8), and His love grows as we abide in fellowship with Him and
love others. "For though we have never yet seen God, when we love each other
God lives in us and *his love within us grows even stronger*" (1 John 4:12 TLB).

*Above all things **have intense and unfailing love for one another.***
—1 Peter 4:8 AMP

Read 1 John 3:17-18, Proverbs 3:27-28, Galatians 6:10, and Luke 6:38.
What do these verses speak to you about expressing love to fellow believers?

Who can you demonstrate this kind of love to? In what specific ways?

*Mostly what God does is love you. Keep company with him and
learn a life of love. Observe how Christ loved us. His love was not
cautious but extravagant. He didn't love in order to get something
from us but to give everything of himself to us. Love like that.*
—Ephesians 5:1-2 The Message

Read Matthew 5:43-47, Romans 12:20-21, and Luke 6:35.
What do these verses speak to you about expressing love to your enemies?

Who in your life can you show this love? How?

Pray for this person, speaking blessings over them that you would like in your own life. Ask God for practical
ways you can demonstrate His love to them. Obey what He says and watch what happens!

Day 5 FOLLOW THE SPIRIT'S LEADING

*Those who belong to Christ Jesus have nailed the passions and desires of their sinful nature to his cross and crucified them there. Since we are living by the Spirit, **let us follow the Spirit's leading** in every part of our lives.*
—Galatians 5:24-25 NLT

Paul's description of the last days in 2 Timothy 3:1-9 reveals that the flesh will dominate many believers' lives. They will be self-centered, proud, and lovers of pleasure instead of lovers of God. The way to avoid falling into this trap is to follow the Holy Spirit's leading. This means learning to say *no* to the world's ways and not following your flesh—what *you* want, what *you* think, and how *you* feel. Well-known evangelist, pastor, and author **Lester Sumrall** said,

"Satan will come in such deceiving ways that many will not recognize him. His devices may seem so innocent, yet they will trap men's spirits so that they will not be able to worship God. This is why *it is so important that we learn to live in our spirit-man and to keep constant and consistent fellowship with God*. We will win in the final battle if, and only if, we live with the spirit as king and Jesus as Lord. By living in the spirit, we become the triumphant church against which the gates of hell cannot prevail. (See Matthew 16:18)."[9]

God says, "If you follow your selfish desires, you will harvest destruction, but if you **follow the Spirit**, you will harvest eternal life" (Galatians 6:8 CEV).

Read each scripture and identify the wisdom you can apply to your life.

To keep from following the *world's ways*, meditate on...

1 John 2:15-17, Titus 2:12-13, and James 4:1-10

Colossians 3:1-4, Galatians 6:14, and Romans 12:2

To help you *follow the Holy Spirit* and keep you from following your *flesh*, meditate on...

Romans 8:1-14

Galatians 5:16-26

Day 6 BE A CHAMPION OF TRUTH!

With God's help we will do mighty things, for he will trample down our foes.
—Psalm 108:13 NLT

In these last days, great adversity will set the stage for a generation of champions to arise, and they will be extraordinary. These believers will not draw back or compromise, but through their tenacious beliefs and actions, they will make great advancements for the Kingdom of God. They will truly distinguish themselves as strong lights for His glory, excelling in all aspects of life. God wants you to be one of these champions!

CHAMPION

According to Noah Webster, a *champion* is "one who fights in his own cause or who undertakes a combat in the place or cause of another." He or she is a "hero, a brave warrior."[10]

Author and pastor **Mark Batterson** confirms the arrival of this new breed of warriors. He states:

"God is raising up a generation of lion chasers that don't just run away from evil. God is raising up a generation of lion chasers that have the courage to compete for the kingdom. ...Lion chasers don't retreat. They attack. Lion chasers aren't reactors. They are creators. Lion chasers refuse to live their lives in a defensive posture. They are actively looking for ways to make a difference."[11]

You have what it takes to never give up—the limitless, matchless power of God's grace! "God will bless you, if you don't give up when your faith is being tested. He will reward you with a glorious life" (James 1:12 CEV). The rewards are for both this life and the one to come.

Read Matthew 6:19-21 and 1 Timothy 6:18-19. What healthy perspective do these verses provide?

_____

_____

_____

God blesses you when you are mocked and persecuted and
lied about because you are my followers. Be happy about it!
Be very glad! For a great reward awaits you in heaven.
—Matthew 5:11-12 NLT

Read Revelation 2:7, 26-28; 3:12, 21; Luke 22:28-29 and 2 Timothy 2:12 and identify the eternal rewards awaiting you if you relentlessly resist the enemy and persevere through trials.

_____

_____

_____

Read Matthew 16:27, Romans 2:6-8, and Revelation 22:12. What truth is repeated regarding our rewards? How does this challenge you, especially in view of 1 Corinthians 3:7-15?

_____

_____

_____

Make no mistake. As a relentless champion of truth, you will be rewarded. God is a rewarder, and He rewards those who diligently seek Him and take Him at His Word (Hebrews 11:6). So "whatever you do, work at it with all your heart, as though you were working for the Lord and not for people. Remember that the Lord will give you as a reward what he has kept for his people. For Christ is the real Master you serve" (Colossians 3:23-24 GNT).

SESSION SUMMARY
In these last days it is difficult to be a Christian, but it is not impossible. God has given you the empowerment of grace to live relentlessly in spite of any opposition or the condition of others in the church. He is well able to keep you in His care. So *continue in the truth* and *don't compromise!* Set your eyes on God's heavenly prize and choose to never give up. The reward for overcoming, both in this life and the next, is far greater than any adversity or hardship you will ever face.

(1) Charles F. Stanley, *Walking Wisely* (Nashville, TN: Thomas Nelson Publishers, 2002) p. 242. (2) Adapted from *Thayer's Greek-English Lexicon of the New Testament*, Joseph H. Thayer (Grand Rapids, MI: Baker Book House Company, 1977) p. 48. (3) Adapted from *Noah Webster's First Edition of an American Dictionary of the English Language* (1828), Republished in facsimile edition by Foundation for American Christian Education (San Francisco, CA 2000). (4) Ibid. (5) See note 2, p. 79. (6) A.W. Tozer, *The Warfare of the Spirit* (Camp Hill, PA: Wing Spread Publishers, 1993) p. 124. (7) Francis Frangipane, *Holiness, Truth and the Presence of God* (Cedar Rapids, IA: Arrow Publications, 1999) p. 55. (8) David Jeremiah, *Living with Confidence in a Chaotic World* (Nashville, TN: Thomas Nelson, 2009) p. 182. (9) Lester Sumrall, *Spirit, Soul, and Body* (New Kensington, PA: Whitaker House, 1995) pp. 251-252. (10) See note 3. (11) Mark Batterson, *In a Pit with a Lion on a Snowy Day* (Colorado Springs, CO: Multnomah Books, 2006) pp. 120-121.

Notes

Notes

Notes

Notes

Notes

Notes

Notes

Notes

Notes

Notes

Notes

When we, as the body of Christ, do what we are called to do, the Spirit empowers us to respond to every need He places before us. We know that the Church carries the divine solution to every human problem. As part of the expression of the global Church, we believe that God has ordained us to proclaim life, hope, and freedom in every corner of the earth. Ephesians 2:10 tells us, "We are God's masterpiece. He has created us anew in Christ Jesus, so we can do the good things he planned for us long ago." (NLT)

As we have prayed and dreamed about these eternal plans, we have refined our efforts into three strategic focuses: teach, reach, and rescue.

So we tell others about Christ, warning everyone and teaching everyone with all the wisdom God has given us.
—Colossians 1:28 NLT

Messenger International always has been and always will be committed to the teaching of life-transforming truth. We are transformed through the power of God's Word, so it is our aim to further equip individuals, churches, and leaders through God-inspired teaching.

Afterward Jesus himself sent them out from east to west with the sacred and unfailing message of salvation that gives eternal life.
—Mark 16:8 NLT

We have a dedicated global focus to make these messages available to pastors and leaders regardless of location or financial position. We support this work through the translation and distribution of our resources in over 60 languages and through our broadcast, "The Messenger," which reaches into over 200 nations.

The LORD replies, "I have seen violence done to the helpless, and I have heard the groans of the poor. Now I will rise up to rescue them, as they have longed for me to do."
—Psalm 12:5 NLT

The Church is His hands and feet to a lost and hurting world. Poverty and the tyranny of human trafficking have imprisoned multiplied millions. Messenger International is committed to rescue, restoration, and empowerment both near and far.

When you donate to Messenger International, your contribution is used to teach, reach, and rescue. Visit our website for information on our goals, current projects, and more.

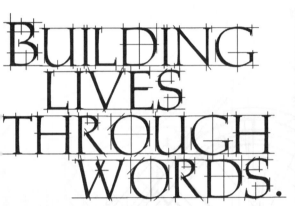

Here's how you can get involved:

Pray
1 John 5:14-15

Give
$50 = 25 books
$100 = 50 books
$1,000 = 500 books

Purchase
Your purchase provides!

Why Books Matter.

It's hard to believe that many people around the world still do not have access to life-transforming resources. The truth is many leaders would risk their lives for books that sit unread on our shelves.

In light of this need Messenger International has made it one of our primary goals to give away more resources than we sell to leaders in developing nations. Join us!

To learn more visit:
MessengerInternational.org

Follow us on Twitter:
@MessengerIntl

teach reach rescue
Messenger International.

THE POWER YOU NEED TO NEVER GIVE UP

RELENTLESS

To get the most out of this message, gather a group or delve into a personal study with the full 12-part curriculum.

This *Relentless* Curriculum is designed to instill perseverance and build your faith. It will help you uncover life-changing truths about tribulation, resistance, and the fulfillment of God's destiny for your life.

The Relentless Experience includes:

- 12 video sessions on 4 DVDs (30 minutes each)
- 12 audio sessions on 6 CDs (30 minutes each)
- *Relentless* Hardcover Book
- Study Guide & Devotional
- *Relentless Experience* Online Resources
- Promotional Materials

Churches & Pastors –

Local churches are the passion and heart of this ministry. Our Church Relations team connects with pastors, churches, and ministry leaders worldwide. It is their joy and honor to encourage leaders, pray for churches, provide life-transforming resources, and build authentic relationships.

USA: 800.648.1477   AUS: 1.300.650.577   UK: 0800.9808.933

RelentlessOnline.org

THE FEAR OF THE LORD
CURRICULUM

Unlock God's Treasures in Your Life...

What is the fear of the Lord? What does it look like? John Bevere reveals from Scripture this often-overlooked and misunderstood life-saving truth. It is the key to wisdom, knowledge, and intimacy with God.

You will be challenged throughout this powerful curriculum to embrace the fear of the Lord in your daily life. If you are ready to grow in your knowledge of God, then this study is for you. Whether used individually or in a group, this riveting message will revolutionize your life!

INCLUDES:
- 8 30-MINUTE VIDEO SESSIONS ON 3 DVDs
- 8 30-MINUTE AUDIO SESSIONS ON 4 CDs
- THE FEAR OF THE LORD BOOK
- DEVOTIONAL WORKBOOK
- PROMOTIONAL MATERIAL TO HELP GATHER GROUPS

INCLUDES:
- 12 30-MINUTE VIDEO SESSIONS ON 4 DVDs
- 12 30-MINUTE AUDIO SESSIONS ON 6 CDs
- HARDCOVER BOOK
- DEVOTIONAL WORKBOOK
- PROMOTIONAL MATERIALS

Extraordinary
CURRICULUM

The *Extraordinary* Curriculum is an extensive journey with 12 video and audio sessions, a thought-provoking devotional workbook, and a hardcover book. As each session builds, you will be positioned to step into the unknown and embrace your divine empowerment.

BREAKING INTIMIDATION
CURRICULUM

Everyone has been intimidated at some point in life. Do you really know why it happened or how to keep it from happening again? John Bevere exposes the root of intimidation, challenges you to break its fearful grip, and teaches you to release God's gifts and establish His dominion in your life.

INCLUDES:
- EIGHT 30-MINUTE VIDEO SESSIONS ON 3 DVDs
- EIGHT 30-MINUTE AUDIO SESSIONS ON 4 CDs
- BREAKING INTIMIDATION BOOK
- DEVOTIONAL WORKBOOK
- PROMOTIONAL MATERIALS

INCLUDES:
- 12 30-MINUTE VIDEO LESSONS ON 4 DVDs
- 12 30-MINUTE AUDIO LESSONS ON 6 CDs
- HONOR'S REWARD HARDCOVER BOOK
- DEVOTIONAL WORKBOOK
- PROMOTIONAL MATERIALS

HONOR'S REWARD
CURRICULUM

This curriculum will unveil the power and truth of an often overlooked principle–Honor. If you understand the vital role of this virtue, you will attract blessing both now and for eternity. This insightful message teaches you how to extend honor to your Creator, family members, authorities and those who surround your world.

THE BAIT OF SATAN
CURRICULUM

Jesus said, "It's impossible that no offenses will come."
–Luke 17:1

A most crucial message for believers in this hour.

"This message is possibly the most important confrontation with truth you'll encounter in your lifetime. The issue of offense – the very core of *The Bait of Satan* – is often the most difficult obstacle an individual must face and overcome."

– John Bevere

INCLUDES:
* 12 30-MINUTE VIDEO LESSONS ON 4 DVDs
* 12 30-MINUTE AUDIO LESSONS ON 6 CDs
* BEST-SELLING BOOK THE BAIT OF SATAN
* DEVOTIONAL WORKBOOK
* PROMOTIONAL MATERIALS

A HEART ABLAZE
CURRICULUM

Jesus has never accepted lukewarmness. Rather, He calls for passion! This message will challenge you to exchange a mediocre relationship with God for a vibrant, fiery one.

INCLUDES:
* 12 30-MINUTE VIDEO LESSONS ON 4 DVDs
* 12 30-MINUTE AUDIO LESSONS ON 6 CDs
* BEST-SELLING BOOK A HEART ABLAZE
* DEVOTIONAL WORKBOOK
* PROMOTIONAL MATERIALS

UNDER COVER
CURRICULUM

Under the shadow of the Almighty, there is liberty, provision and protection. Unfortunately, many don't understand how to find this secret place. In this curriculum you will learn how biblical submission differs from obedience. You will also learn the distinction between direct and delegated authority and how to respond to and overcome unfair treatment.

INCLUDES:
* 12 30-MINUTE VIDEO LESSONS ON 4 DVDs
* 12 30-MINUTE AUDIO LESSONS ON 6 CDs
* BEST-SELLING BOOK UNDER COVER
* DEVOTIONAL WORKBOOK
* PROMOTIONAL MATERIALS

DRIVEN *by* Eternity
CURRICULUM

Making Your Life Count Today & Forever

We were made for eternity. This life on earth is but a vapor. Yet too many live as though there is nothing on the other side. Scriptural laws and principles may be applied to achieve success on earth, but are we prepared for eternity? This power-packed teaching, including an allegory on the Kingdom of Affabel, will help you understand that the choices you make today will determine how you spend eternity.

INCLUDES:
* 12 40-MINUTE VIDEO LESSONS ON 4 DVDs
* DRIVEN BY ETERNITY HARDCOVER BOOK
* WORKBOOK & DEVOTIONAL
* AFFABEL AUDIO THEATER

DRAWING NEAR

CURRICULUM

Drawing extensively from his own journey, John has specially written and prepared this *Drawing Near* message to lead you into times of private and intimate communion with God Himself. This devotional kit acts as a treasure map, guiding you around potential pitfalls and breaking through personal barriers, leading you into new and glorious realms of a lifelong adventure with God!

INCLUDES:
- 12 30-MINUTE VIDEO LESSONS ON 4 DVDs
- BEST-SELLING BOOK DRAWING NEAR
- 84-DAY DEVOTIONAL
- WORKBOOK

RESCUED

2 hours on 2 CDs

From the novel *Rescued*

A trapped father. A desperate son. A clock ticking down toward certain death and a fate even more horrible still...

For Alan Rockaway, his teenaged son Jeff, and his new bride Jenny, it's

been little more than a leisurely end to a week-long cruise...a horrifying crash and even more, a plunge toward the unknown...Everything Alan has assumed about himself is flipped upside down. In the ultimate rescue operation, life or death is just the beginning!

AFFABEL
WINDOW OF ETERNITY

2.5 hours on 4 CDs

FEATURING JOHN RHYS-DAVIES AND A CAST OF HOLLYWOOD ACTORS

AN EPIC AUDIO THEATER PORTRAYING THE REALITY OF THE JUDGMENT SEAT OF CHRIST. GET READY TO BE CHANGED FOREVER...AND PREPARE FOR ETERNITY!

This audio dramatization, taken from John Bevere's book, *Driven by Eternity*, will capture your heart and soul as you experience life on "the other side" where eternity is brought into the present and all must stand before the Great King and Judge. Be prepared for a roller coaster ride of joy, sorrow, astonishment, and revelation as lifelong rewards are bestowed on some while others are bound hand and foot and cast into outer darkness by the Royal Guard!

BOOKS BY JOHN

Messenger International.
teach reach rescue

Messenger International exists to help individuals, families, churches, and nations realize and experience the transforming power of God's Word. This realization will result in lives empowered, communities transformed, and a dynamic response to the injustices plaguing our world.

UNITED STATES
P.O. Box 888
Palmer Lake, CO
80133-0888
800-648-1477 (US & Canada)
Tel: 719-487-3000
mail@MessengerInternational.org

AUSTRALIA
Rouse Hill Town Centre
P.O. Box 6444
Rouse Hill NSW 2155
In AUS: 1-300-650-577
Tel: +61 2 9679 4900
australia@MessengerInternational.org

EUROPE
P.O. Box 1066
Hemel, Hempstead HP2 7GQ
United Kingdom
In UK: 0800 9808 933
Tel: +44 1442 288 531
europe@MessengerInternational.org

The Messenger television program broadcasts in over 200 countries. Please check your local listings for day and time.

www.MessengerInternational.org

Follow John & Lisa Bevere on **facebook**. & **twitter** for updates & information on meetings.